The NEW Low-Maintenance Garden

The NEW Low-Maintenance Garden

How to Have a
Beautiful, Productive
Garden and the
Time to Enjoy It

• • •

Valerie Easton

PHOTOGRAPHY BY Jacqueline M. Koch

TIMBER PRESS
PORTLAND   LONDON

Frontispiece: This starkly modern terrace is softened with one big pot stuffed with rosettes of Canary Island aeonium (*Aeonium canariense*) that play beautifully off the fluffy leaves of the African fern pine (*Afrocarpus gracilior*). These two plants make a striking statement yet are easy to care for because both require the same conditions of sun and drought. Sekhri garden, Jeong Hyeon Lee design, San Francisco, CA.

Copyright © 2009 by Valerie Easton and Jacqueline M. Koch.

Published in 2009 by Timber Press, Inc.

The Haseltine Building
133 S.W. Second Avenue, Suite 450
Portland, Oregon 97204-3527
www.timberpress.com

2 The Quadrant
135 Salusbury Road
London NW6 6RJ
www.timberpress.co.uk

Mention of trademark, proprietary product, or vendor does not constitute a guarantee or warranty of the product by the publisher or author and does not imply its approval to the exclusion of other products or vendors.

Printed in the United States of America
Second printing 2010

Library of Congress Cataloging-in-Publication Data
Easton, Valerie.
The new low-maintenance garden : how to have a beautiful, productive garden and the time to enjoy it / Valerie Easton ; photography by Jacqueline M. Koch. — 1st ed.
     p. cm.
Includes bibliographical references and index.
ISBN 978-0-88192-916-4
ISBN 978-1-60469-166-5 (pbk.)
1. Low maintenance gardening. 2. Landscape gardening. 3. Gardens—Design. I. Koch, Jacqueline. II. Title. III. Title: New low maintenance garden. IV. Title: How to have a beautiful, productive garden and the time to enjoy it.
SB473.E235 2009
635—dc22
                              2009008199

A catalog record for this book is also available from the British Library

Book design: Karen Schober, Seattle, Washington

*To my nongardening family, who by enjoying the garden
in their own ways have taught me the breadth of its pleasures.
Their disinclination to pick up a shovel led to my simplifying the
garden so that I'm able to care for it joyously and by myself.*

−VALERIE EASTON

*Always to my mother, who first got me into
the garden, and to Chris, who keeps the garden of
my life abundant, rich, and full of discovery.*

−JACQUELINE M. KOCH

Contents

Acknowledgments

I'M GRATEFUL TO MY PARTNER IN PUBLISHING, Jacqueline Koch, who tracked down so many of the gardeners and designers you meet in these pages. Her photographic artistry makes the book. Thanks to all the hard-working folks at Timber Press, especially Tom Fischer, whose early interest kicked this project into gear. I never would have considered doing another book if he hadn't promised us the design skills of Karen Schober, whose vision and talent light up our work.

Writing a column in the age of email is an interactive endeavor, and I'm grateful to all the readers who have responded to my weekly "Plant Life" column in the *Seattle Times* over the past dozen years. Your enthusiasm keeps me gardening and writing.

Most of all, I thank the gardeners and designers who so generously share their creativity and knowledge in these pages. The idea of a simplified, "new" low-maintenance garden may have started in my own backyard, but it grew in the writing to encompass so many innovative gardens around the country. Thanks, too, to the many experts who shared their thoughts on the future of gardening. I hope you're as inspired by their humor, prescience, and collective wisdom as I am.

VALERIE EASTON

THIS SMALL SPACE ON THE PAGE WON'T ALLOW ME to name all the invaluable friends, garden owners, designers, hortisexuals, landscape architects, artists, and indefatigable garden enthusiasts who helped make this project possible. I hope you know who you are and that you have my gratitude.

JACQUELINE M. KOCH

Ribbons of orange, repeated in pots, pansies, and wallflowers, weave through my garden to warm it up in all seasons. An egg-shaped orange pot sports 'Princess Irene' tulips in spring, followed by foliage plants dotted with apricot pansies in summer.

The Simplified Garden: A New Low-Maintenance Manifesto

GARDENING, LIKE EVERYTHING ELSE WORTHWHILE IN LIFE except maybe love, comes down to time and resources. Our passion for plants and nature too often obscures this basic truth. But we ignore the time and resource part of the equation at our peril.

The idea for a fresh take on a simplified, low-maintenance garden came directly from my own years of intensely gardening an overplanted quarter-acre hillside. All the weeding, grooming, watering, mulching, and mowing finally wore me out. As a horticultural librarian and weekly garden columnist for the *Seattle Times*, I used my garden as my laboratory. For many years my enthusiasm for digging, planting, and caring for all I'd created was boundless. And then one day it wasn't.

The spring I felt more jaded than enthused when I looked at flats of beguiling baby annuals waiting to be potted up, I realized with a sinking heart that while my passion for plants and gardens was perpetual, my inclination to spend most waking moments working outdoors was not.

And then my husband resigned as yard boy. After thirty years of marriage, he'd run out of patience helping me with something he was never much interested in.

OPPOSITE and ABOVE: My garden in late summer is rich in coneflowers, nasturtiums, and pumpkins. Lemon verbena is in the foreground; the second bed is trimmed with a chive hedge.

As middle-age crises go, it wasn't too bad. He simply told me, again and again until I heard him, that he was going to spend his weekends bike riding and kayaking rather than hauling buckets of mulch up the stairs, mucking out the pond, and carting away excess biomass. Greg now claims it took four years before I heard him say he was through toiling in the garden. Out of kindness, he kept working during the time it took to sink into my consciousness that I no longer had a crew. When I finally did understand that I was on my own caring for these thousands of plants, I belatedly realized that while I loved my garden, I too craved a little downtime, more spaces in my life to read a novel, go to a movie, or browse a museum without feeling guilty about time away from endless garden chores. It was time for a new low-maintenance garden intervention.

And It Wasn't Just Me

A great pleasure of my job as a garden writer is spending time in other people's gardens and hearing their stories. About the same time I was reaching my own epiphany, I realized more and more gardeners I spoke with complained of weariness as often as they bubbled with enthusiasm. Nursery profits are slipping, and plant show attendance is down all over the country, and not just because of the unpredictable weather.

Plants grow large and trees mature. Water is scarcer and more expensive. Our reverence for the earth grows stronger as we realize how human impact, including gardening practices, has brought on scary climate change. Gardens grow rooty and shady while those of us who tend them grow older. But it was more than just tired backs and a fresh environmental ethos going on here—I found younger gardeners, too, who wanted a beautiful, productive garden and were seeking ways to simplify their outdoor spaces.

New generations of gardeners don't have the time to spend cosseting plants and devoting their weekends to yard work. They may appreciate a pretty garden as a place to entertain, or love to pick lettuce and tomatoes fresh from the garden, but they're busy with family, work, and friendships. How to balance growing food and flowers with full-time jobs, children, and a social life?

Many of the twenty- and thirty-something gardeners I talk with have much to teach us longtime, plant-besotted gardeners. While the upcoming generations

"I think that we are simplifying our lives and that modern gardens are a reflection of the desire for a saner, more-ordered world."

–Lucy Hardiman, garden designer

of gardeners love plants, too, they tend to focus their energies on creating outdoor spaces for dining, play, relaxation, and entertaining. Many are determined to grow vegetables and fruit in however much garden space they can eke out in the current housing market, be it on a deck or balcony or in a courtyard or neighborhood

Raised beds built of inexpensive split-faced CMUs (concrete masonry units) hold an assortment of cut-and-come-again lettuces. Galvanized steel feed troughs are four feet across, large enough to hold a medley of useful plants, including a bay tree, a columnar apple tree, strawberries, tomatoes, zinnias, and Peruvian lilies. Rainwater can percolate through the gravel ground cover, and flowers seed in for a casual look.

P-patch. These newer gardeners grew up with farmers' markets and know fresh when they taste it. They're savvy about organics and the threat to our food supply. Luckily, there are so many ornamental vegetables, fruits, and herbs available now, there's no trade-off involved—you can have your garden and eat it too.

The Feast We Forget to Partake Of

The ancient concept of garden as sanctuary has been rediscovered in our busy, overcrowded, techie world, creating a shift in our gardening consciousness. Somewhere along the way to plant collecting and competitive gardening, we forgot the ancient notion of the garden as a place of respite, an oasis remote from worldly cares and chores. We forgot nature's ability to soothe, renew, and nurture humans as it does the rest of the living creatures on earth. We've thought of nature as something to prune, control, mow, and trim, overlooking to our detriment her timeless role as antidote to the stresses and strains of the world. Nature's ability to work her magic on us is dependent on our slowing down and looking closely, not on our constant efforts to improve upon her.

As the pace of life grows faster, the world noisier, and prices for everything higher, we turn to our outdoor spaces as a dose of stress relief, a place to relax with friends and family, and for quiet contemplation of weather, beauty, the passing of the seasons. You needn't pay outrageous gas prices or waste hours commuting when your destination is right outside your back door. Our gardens are all too often the feast we forget to partake of.

How is it possible to achieve a feeling of peace and relaxation if we're always digging, weeding, fussing, working? How to enjoy what a garden can offer if we never take a moment to look up from the task at hand? When I was growing up, every Saturday morning we kids had to choose between indoor or outdoor chores. I always picked vacuuming and dusting, because even at the ages of eight and ten and twelve, it was very clear to me that garden work was endless and I'd never finish up if I chose to help my mom in her garden.

So how to escape the fugue of garden work? How can a garden be designed and planted to offer respite to the one who cares for it as well as friends and family? How can we create something beautiful and rewarding yet not spend more energy and time than we have available? These are the questions I kept asking

OPPOSITE: 'Scarlet Sentinel' columnar apples ripen nestled into a raised bed planted with Peruvian lilies (*Alstroemeria* spp.), which are especially long-blooming flowers ideal for flower arranging.

"Does it really matter whether it's a 'modern design' or not? More important is whether a garden connects one to the earth, feeding the soul and soothing the mind."

–Suzy Bales, author

myself as I considered my own fatigue and heard the same weary lament from so many other gardeners.

I set a new goal, one that seemed nearly impossible at the outset of my gardening odyssey. I wanted to be able to look out my window and see more than just work waiting for me out there. I wanted to enjoy my garden, not just labor in

it. Was it possible to grow the flowers that I love—I came to gardening originally because of a passion for flower arranging—plus berries, vegetables, herbs, and lettuces without again creating a garden that ceaselessly called for more care than I had time or energy to give it?

Raised beds do double duty in my small garden, providing topography, privacy for a little corner terrace, and a warm, well-drained environment for growing edibles and ornamentals.

What's a New Low-Maintenance Garden?

The term *low-maintenance gardening* doesn't exactly bring to mind the lush, sensual, productive garden most of us long for. In fact, *low-maintenance* must be among the least exciting couplings of words ever written or uttered. What gardener isn't scornful of beauty bark, expanses of static evergreens, blanket spraying, or whatever dismal picture *low-maintenance* brings to mind? Any garden worth the name takes work, and to pretend otherwise must be deceptive or ignorant, yes?

And yet we need to come to terms with our own time and energy versus the garden of our dreams. I suggest that a simplified, new low-maintenance garden is the route to truly enjoying your garden again, now and in the future. A simplified garden, thoughtfully planned, can be just as rewarding as a more complicated, labor-intensive one. There's every bit as much wonder to be found in a more intimately scaled garden.

Most of the plants in my garden grow in raised beds. The exception is the small, colorful border next to the main terrace, with orange wallflowers, heuchera, and ornamental grasses. The little water feature provides water music and attracts birds.

Just to put to rest those nasty images in your mind—new low-maintenance gardens aren't landscapes thrown into the ground by crews blitzing through homogenized developments. Nor are they yards created by people who tend to park trucks on their front lawns.

Rather, new low-maintenance gardens are easy to live with and live in. They're thoughtful spaces for outdoor living as well as plants, tailored to the needs of the people who create and use them. New low-maintenance gardens might be rich in flowers for cutting, feature places for kids to play, consist of a few pots or a luscious vegetable garden. Most often they're on the small side, even though they might well be part of a much larger piece of property.

While new low-maintenance gardens are as various as climate, topography, personal needs, and aesthetics can make them, they also have much in common. First and foremost, new low-maintenance gardens are defined by careful, thoughtful choices and decisive editing. They have a minimum of lawn, little dividing or pruning to be done, and no spraying, staking, or topiary. Most often plants are placed where they can grow to their own natural sizes and shapes without interference.

New low-maintenance gardens are comfortable in size and scale. They offer places to relax, to play, to eat and nap. Most are neither manicured nor scruffy, but maintained at a state somewhere in between that might be called lived-in, relaxed, or better yet, inviting. They appeal to the senses with fragrance, color, water, and art.

New low-maintenance gardens are especially reflective of the gardeners who make them, because they're made with such care and attention. Careful, considered choices and editing ensure that every inch of ground and hour of work is as rewarding as possible. Most of all, they don't awaken dread in their owners at the thought of caring for them.

Not "Gardening Lite"

New low-maintenance gardens aren't "gardening lite." Hours of toil and tasks may be left out of the recipe, yet these gardens aren't deficient in nourishment. The exhaustion is taken out, not the fulfillment. This less-labor-intensive way of crafting gardens doesn't remove the essence of the garden. Unlike cardboard

"Modern gardeners savor a special attention to detail, to distinctions, to all things natural, to the art of living."

—Alice Doyle, proprietor of Loghouse Plants

Downsizing doesn't mean foregoing the joys of fragrant foliage or fresh berries warmed by the sun. Raspberries and fragrant-leafed geraniums mingle in one of the raised beds.

cookies or gummy fake cheese, these are full-bodied, nutrient-rich gardens—not merely creations that might look like gardens but fail to offer all the satisfactions. New low-maintenance gardens offer beauty to feed your eyes, flowers to fill your house, fruit and vegetables to fill your family and friends' bellies and maybe even enough to fill their fridges—but they don't wear you out along the way.

Analogies can be made on nearly every level. Architecturally, new low-maintenance gardens bring to mind Mies van der Rohe's "less is more" minimalism, yet there's a decided element of Shaker or Asian integrity and simplicity. In clothing, think Levi 501s with a black T-shirt or turtleneck and boots, loafers, or sneakers, or whatever your equivalent of such classy comfort clothes might be. In art, perhaps a Rothko or Wyeth painting would be analogous, as opposed to a Gaugin or Van Gogh. When it comes to food, the analog might be a rich, crusty mac-and-cheese with a simple fresh green salad finished off with a slice of chocolate cake or a blackberry crisp (depending on the season), satisfying foods with visceral richness yet basic goodness.

What it comes down to is that new low-maintenance gardens are about so much more than plants. Perhaps because we formed our visions of gardens by reading gorgeous British gardening tomes, we tend to idealize flowery estate gardens, vast expanses of croquet lawns, or packed-in, ever-changing herbaceous borders. Such models make a goal of low maintenance seem scarcely possible.

We usually start our gardens with the best intentions and often with a plan in mind, which is soon abandoned when we tote home black nursery pot after nursery pot. All those tiny trees and shrubs and baby perennials look so innocent and scarcely dangerous. Just squeeze one more in, and then another and another. Soon enough our garden becomes a conglomeration of plants we've fallen in love with. We end up with a space that isn't particularly personal or reflective of our needs, as well as such a maintenance nightmare we don't love it for long. We're always saying, if just to ourselves, "If only this bed was weeded/finished/cleaned up." We're never at peace or satisfied with what we've created, because we just can't keep up with all those plants. If you come to gardening through your love of plants, and most of us do, how can you possibly create a non-plant-centered garden?

That's the essential challenge. Limited time and resources, as well as changing weather patterns, make it smart if not imperative to find new, more sustainable models of gardening. And let's face it—no matter how large a garden you have, you can't grow everything anyway. So why not make wise choices to grow just what best suits your tastes, climate, and topography, and that you can care for with ease? Or relative ease, anyway.

I probably took the simplest route to a new low-maintenance garden—we sold our house with big garden the week our son graduated from high school. And I started over. I was so excited about the idea of creating a brand new kind of garden I hardly brought a single plant with me from my old garden. I was ready to downsize, to start fresh after so many years of gardening the same plot. Friends, neighbors, and readers of my column seemed much more nostalgic about my garden and saddened by the change than I was. I looked forward to a whole new style of gardening.

Starting Over: Decisions and Practicalities

My husband and I moved to a small house with a very small garden in the seaside village of Langley, on Whidbey Island, a half-hour drive and short ferry ride north of Seattle.

My hope was to make a new low-maintenance garden that wouldn't look it. Gravel ground cover and raised beds eliminate weeding and soil and drainage problems while making it easy to reach and care for the plants.

The tiny L-shaped garden was inauspicious at best. Perhaps only because my old garden was so rich in views, hillsides, and rockeries, I delighted in this flat, featureless space. I could in all good conscience rip out the ratty lawn and struggling, undistinguished trees and start from scratch in search of the elusive goal of a simplified, low-maintenance garden.

I knew I wanted to create a garden for entertaining friends and family. I wanted a garden geared to summer and autumn, which is when we have our driest weather in the Northwest so spend most time outdoors. Just because we *can* garden most months of the year doesn't mean we have to, and I decided that one of the best ways to make the most of a small garden space is to emphasize plants for summer and autumn. I wanted to inject some cool design and architectural elements into the garden, build a little topography into this narrow, flat little space. I wanted raised beds to grow berries, herbs, lettuces, and flowers, and plenty of patio space for dining and sitting. I wanted the garden to feel spacious and open despite its small size.

I knew I didn't want an overplanted naturalistic garden or a thirsty, greedy, maintenance-heavy lawn. I was determined not to create another garden that cried out for attention so loudly I never had a minute when I didn't feel its need. How to make a garden so very different from any I'd had before?

I began with a central organizing concept to help me make the tough choices necessary to end up with a truly low-maintenance garden. Years ago I wrote a book about how visual artists go about garden making (*Artists in Their Gardens*, written with David Laskin) and remain fascinated by the fact that these artists always had a concept firmly in mind as they designed and worked in their gardens. The artists started with an idea of how they wanted their gardens to feel and look, and every decision served this concept as they set about molding outdoor space. Plants weren't the first and most important part of making a garden but rather a creative medium like any other, albeit a dynamic one that grew and changed during the seasons. Whether an outdoor sculpture gallery, a Zen retreat, or a quirky courtyard, each artist's garden had a cohesion and harmony I greatly admired.

I started with a simple concept, as befitted the kind of garden I hoped to create. I thought about the warm, walled area around many English houses, used for sitting and dining outside, for growing food and flowers. Outside these sheltering

"The modern landscape has followed the freeing of the contraptions of society at large; no more ties and tiaras, an acknowledgment and understanding of the full diversity of the human experience, aka more honesty."

–Dan Hinkley, author and plant explorer

A shallow metal tray on top of a potting bench is a miniature green roof, a fun project undertaken to learn just how little soil is needed to grow grasses and sedum. Turns out they made it through the winter in a scant two inches of soil heaped up around a few beach stones.

It took a glue gun, a bag of moss, and some paint to transform a rickety old chair into a garden focal point.

walls lay the rest of the estate. I'd skip the estate part and emulate the intimate garden closely connected to the house, using modern materials rather than mossy old brick walls. I wanted the garden to feel intimate, sheltered, and comfortable. I chose utilitarian materials that suited its agrarian setting in a casual little village with sheep and cow pastures right across the street.

With the concept firmly in mind, I knew I needed help with geometry and architecture. I also needed guidance in planning for an adequate amount of open space. I knew my habit of planting every possible inch of ground all too well. Designer Richard Hartlage sketched out the diamond-shaped main terrace, tall curved screens, and diagonal grid of raised beds that define the finished garden and visually widen the narrow space. My architect daughter worked out the proportions of the raised beds and did the schematic, to-scale drawings. I hired landscapers to rip out the lawn, lay down landscape fabric, build the raised beds, haul in good dirt and gravel. Carpenters enlarged the deck and built the gates and two tall cedar-and-hog-wire screens.

Very early in the process I chose a color scheme, figuring a realistic way to narrow down plant choices was to work with a very few colors. How better to keep the number and variety of plants under control than to grow only what I love best in a narrow range of colors? This way I'd never feel plant-deprived, because I'd have plenty of my favorite butter yellow, chartreuse, plum, and orange. These four basic colors are repeated throughout the garden, from ground level to trees, in foliage and flower. Their warmth helps counteract our cool, cloudy weather. The dramatic contrast of pale, bright, and deep colors enlivens a garden paved in concrete and gravel.

To reinforce and remind me to stick to these four colors, I commissioned mosaic pavers from Vashon Island artist Clare Dohna. I sent her color chips, and she created three intricate and lively pavers to be set right into the patios. I wanted her art to be part of the very fabric of the garden. The plum, marigold, leaf green, and soft yellow in her designs set the color palette for all that followed.

I can't imagine a garden without water's sound and reflection but had learned from my last garden how much work a pond is. I loved madly that pond's fountain, its reflectiveness, how it attracted birds and creatures to the garden . . . but regretted the pond in almost equal proportion. I didn't relish the thought of ever again pulling on boots in March to climb down into chilly water to muck out the

As flowers bloom and fade, the garden's color scheme is reinforced throughout the year by pots, fabrics, and a serene little orange Buddha made from weatherproof resin.

pond. So I chose a sandstone fountain that needs only to be filled with water and plugged in. Placed on the main terrace next to the dining table, the fountain creates maximum water effect with the sound and movement of its water and without much work or bother. What I didn't realize was that bees, birds, butterflies, and dragonflies would be attracted to such a small volume of water just as much as to a pond. I haven't missed the old pond for a minute.

The garden is built and paved with concrete, gravel, wood, and metal—all humble and unadorned materials that suit the little house, its setting, and my budget. The screens are built of hog wire framed in pressure-treated lumber wrapped with cedar. Raised beds are a combination of round galvanized metal feed troughs and rectangular split-faced concrete block. All the gray creates a calm oasis for art and the explosion of carefully contained, exuberant plantings. How in the world to choose just three trees and squeeze in vital plantings for color, food, and fragrance, like the sweet peas, strawberries, hydrangeas, and lilies I couldn't do without? It was all a matter of planting only a few of what I love most. I remembered my yoga teacher repeating that freedom comes only through discipline, a maxim as true for gardening as for yoga.

Restricting plant choices to a handful of trees, three kinds of hydrangea, and a minimum of perennials was kind of like realizing, in my case quite far along in life, that I can't take home every darling puppy or kitten I see. I've managed to replace unbridled plant lust with plant discipline and have been rewarded with a garden that's sensual but not squeezed, fragrant but not overwhelming. I've ended up with mostly colored foliage, small shrubs, bulbs, edibles, and a few perennials for cutting and seasonal change. And best of all, it's a garden I can care for myself in the time I want to give it. I have time to tinker around with the garden, play around with container plantings, change out plantings. I no longer feel like all I'm doing is working full blast at hard and dirty chores.

Not that I haven't made mistakes, despite a strong concept and determination to cut way down on maintenance. I planted a hedge of the more compact version of Mexican orange (*Choisya ternata* 'Aztec Pearl') along the fence line, thinking it would be easy to keep trimmed to scale. What a delusion that was! It grew lanky, flopped, and took over the bed in only a couple of years. Now the choisya is growing happily in my neighbor's garden, where it can stretch out to its natural size

"The most modern thing about modern gardens is the appearance and feeling of effortlessness. Let it happen. It is such a relief to be freed of fuss."

–Tom Hobbs, author, designer, proprietor of Southlands Nursery

and shape. I've replaced it with a hedge of dwarf conifers (*Taxus baccata* 'Stricta Aurea') tipped with lovely golden-orange needles. Tidy fluffs of sedge are planted around and in between the little trees until they grow, slowly, to fill in against the fence. I've taken out a couple of roses that proved too needy, settling on just one exuberantly healthy and prolific 'Westerland', an apricot-orange climber growing up one of the hog-wire screens. The gravel driveway takes more maintenance time than I'd imagined, but I enjoy its crunch and casual look. I've bought a flame weeder to make weeding more fun and effective, and remain committed to the permeable surface despite its sprouting more weeds than expected.

The Art of the Edit

Four years into the quest for a new way to garden, my island property is lush, productive, fragrant, and colorful. When my children visit, they go outside first to pick berries and lettuces, to check to see if the tomatoes are ripe and which herbs might inspire a dish for dinner. The trees have grown large enough so they create a canopy over shade-loving small shrubs. The hydrangeas and the single lilac bloom prolifically, and my only hosta, 'Sum and Substance', stretches its fat-ribbed leaves across an entire corner of the garden. (If you have room for only one, choose this chartreuse goliath so you get a full dose of hosta.) Friends gather around the outdoor table for iced tea or a meal, and most months of the year I can fill the rooms of the house with foliage and flowers from the garden. Best of all, when I look out the window I don't just see work and more work waiting for me. The photos in this chapter, all taken in my garden, show what I see instead.

Four years have given me perspective on what elements of the garden have turned out to be truly low-maintenance. I can see now which decisions made all the difference between a garden that relieves stress and one that creates it. These are the pieces of the garden that have proved most effective in cutting down on maintenance:

- Size matters. A small garden takes a minimum of resources and time to care for.
- Very little of the garden is actually planted in the ground. Most of the area is taken up with pavers, gravel laid over a layer of landscape cloth, or raised beds, so weeding is kept to a minimum and plants are easier to water and fertilize.
- The "shed garden" is screened off from the rest of the garden. This utility area

Lilies and *Gallardia* 'Oranges and Lemons' in the feed trough frame the central terrace. Both kinds of flowers are colorful and showy; both are easy care, dependable perennials.

holds a toolshed, green cones for recycling kitchen waste, and compost bins, with plenty of out-of-sight storage space for the wheelbarrow and out-of-season pots and paraphernalia.

- Every inch of soil, whether in the ground, raised beds, or pots, has been improved with compost, manure, and mulch, so plants thrive with less intervention.

- The raised beds have a simple drip irrigation system on a timer, and this is where I start seeds and grow edibles, sweet peas, delphiniums, dahlias, and any other plant that needs babying along with frequent watering.

- The two tall, cedar-framed hog-wire screens take advantage of vertical space while saving horizontal space. And I'll admit that the screens are a great way to pack more plants into minimum space. Last summer we could barely see the glint of metal screen beneath the clematis vines, climbing rose, sasanqua camellias, sweet peas, and pumpkins that clamber over the vertical surface. In winter, the bare screens look clean and architectural.

- I grow very few perennials, and the chosen few were carefully vetted to make sure they're long-blooming, look good in bud and in decline, work well in arrangements, and don't need frequent dividing. The deep dark masterwort (*Astrantia major* 'Hadspen Blood'), burgundy knautia (*Knautia macedonica*), dwarf apricot crocosmia (*Crocosmia* 'Solfatare'), autumnal-toned sneezeweed (*Helenium autumnale*), and various heuchera, euphorbia, sedums, and hardy geraniums made the cut.

- The hedge along the fence is clumping bamboo that doesn't travel (*Fargesia robusta*) so needs no more maintenance than fertilizing and thinning once a year, along with regular watering.

- Most of the plants were chosen for their long-lasting foliar effect. Colored, variegated, oversized, and toothed leaves add impact to the garden in most months of the year.

- Most important, the garden has plenty of places to eat, nap, read, and relax— activities in which, for the first time in my gardening life, I actually have time to participate.

What's Modern Now

We're gardening in the new millennium, though you'd never know it by looking at our gardens. We mostly garden as our grandparents did, albeit with a far greater palette of plants and maybe fewer straight rows. Still, our practices and thoughts about gardens remain remarkably static despite the ever-accelerating rate of change around us. There's something comforting in this, perhaps, but we need to face up to the realities of less time and more stress as well as volatile weather, less water, and higher prices for land, housing, and everything else . . . which brings us to the idea that truly modern gardens are about far more than design.

Genuinely modern gardens aren't just spaces garnished with contemporary art or built with aggressive architectural elements. They aren't necessarily minimalist, austere, hard-edged, or galleries for abstract sculpture. Earthworks or stainless steel may look fresh and exciting to the eye, but that doesn't mean the gardens they define are modern.

It's the essence of a garden that defines its modernity, not its style, materials, or ornamentation. Naturalistic gardens uniquely born of their specific locations are modern, as are gardens rich in native plants that nurture and protect living creatures. On this troubled earth, a gardener's respect and reverence for the soil, plants, birds, bees, and butterflies in his or her care matter far more than what the garden looks like. Organic, sustainable gardens are the new avant-garde. So is growing your own food, composting, water catchment and recycling. Not depleting our own or the earth's energies as we garden is the most modern, and eminently reachable, of ideas.

What were once just theories and hopes for an easier, sustainable, more modern way to garden are now a reality for me and for many others around the country. In the pages of this book, you'll hear the words and see the work of gardeners breaking ground along the path to creating a whole new ethos of simplified, new low-maintenance gardens. You'll find more ideas in the "Keep It Simple" section near the end of each chapter.

Though we've done our best to convey the stories of innovative gardeners, there's too much going on out there to capture fully between the pages of any one book. So every chapter ends with a "Resources" section containing what I hope are engagingly short lists of my very favorite books and Web sites to inspire and guide you in your journey to create a more satisfying, rewarding, earth-friendly garden that takes no more time and resources than you have available to give it.

OPPOSITE: Pavers used as stepping stones lead from the garden's main terrace to the utility area. The flamboyant red flower spikes *Lobelia tupa* spill across the pavers. *Daphne* x*transatlantica* 'Summer Ice' is on the left, and in the background are the big, dark leaves of *Ligularia dentata* 'Othello'.

With all this atmosphere, who misses the plants? California designer Cevan Forristt's gardens are about relaxing and entertaining rather than weeding and watering.

Design with Maintenance in Mind

WHERE PLANTS RULE, GARDENERS TOIL. And toil, and toil.

When it comes to effective low-maintenance, it's all about design. It's the design, plus hardscape and architectural elements, that determines how easy any garden is to care for. Without strong, well-thought-out design elements, don't even bother to put those plants in the ground, for you'll be creating a maintenance nightmare for yourself.

Why are gardeners afraid of design? There's a mystique about it that intimidates us, when in fact we can and should be involved in designing our own gardens. Your fingerprints should be all over your garden's design, whether or not you use the services of a landscape architect or garden designer. Gardeners themselves best know and understand what kind of garden will serve their needs and satisfy them in the long run. And gardens that take less time and fewer resources to care for are the most satisfying of all.

If you design your garden one plant at a time, walking around with plastic nursery pot in hand trying to figure out where to put your most current impulse acquisition, you're just making more work for yourself. Throwing more plants at a

"Modern gardens are about spaces that inspire. I want a garden to be joyous, contained by bold architecture, and intelligently usable. I want it to be well considered in its design, but not self-conscious."

–Richard Hartlage, garden designer and author

problem area only makes it more problematic. Take it from one who has learned this lesson the hard way.

Design isn't dependent on style or cost. It's about long-term goals and daily needs. Good design is all about making the choices that will simplify your garden.

Some of the loveliest gardens I've ever seen are simple, intimate spaces that beautifully serve the needs of the gardener and family who live in them. It matters not at all where you live, how big or small your garden or budget, or what style of house and garden you have. Whether you prefer to shape your outdoor space around the plants you love best, tie it to the architecture of the house, or create a world apart, a garden that doesn't scream out for care and attention depends on its design.

A Mantra to Design By

Strong design will carry your garden through the seasons, whether you're a plant collector, an art collector, or just want comfortable outdoor spaces for your family to enjoy. Here's the mantra: Design before plants, think geometry, and invest in infrastructure.

DESIGN BEFORE PLANTS Design elements, such as arbors, decks, patios, and pathways, define and shape space; they create a framework for outdoor living that can then be planted. All plants, from ground-hugging carpeters to trees to the blowsiest of perennials, look best and are easiest to care for when contained, massed, or combined with architectural or structural elements. Put a plant in a pot and it shines. Plant it next to a corner of the house and you notice it. Put a clean metal or wooden edge on a curved bed and it pleases your eye.

Plants are change agents, budding, blooming, fruiting, leafing out, dying down, growing large through the seasons and the years. We choose evergreens for their unchanging looks, but even evergreens are in constant flux. They grow and spread, losing and replacing leaves or needles throughout the year, just as a dog sheds and grows fur. This is why you're better off relying on architectural elements and hardscape to carry your garden through the seasons.

Putting design first reminds plant lovers that gardens are for people. Providing places to stroll, relax, read, nap, and eat outdoors ensures that our gardens are vital, well-used places. And it just so happens that nice wide pathways, generously scaled terraces, patios, and decks, and hunky arbors for shade and privacy make the garden not only more livable but also far easier to care for.

THINK GEOMETRY Geometry is the yin to the yang of plants. The basic shapes of square, rectangle, diamond, and circle are endlessly variable and satisfying in the garden. They ground the garden, create scale, and lend structure and an edge to all the biomass. Circles are especially pleasing in the garden, their softer, more

Garden designer Shirley Watts used a minimum of materials to great effect in the Pleasure garden. Silk roses pattern the blue polycarbonate cabana; underfoot is the crunch and pattern of tumbled old dishes used as ground cover.

Strong geometric shapes of rectilinear patios and raised ponds contrast with globelike pots and boulders to lend a modern vibe to a steep hillside garden planted mostly in natives.

"What's in: clean lines in design, minimal but dynamic plantings, outdoor rooms with all the creature comforts that extend the useable living space. What's out: English perennial borders, cottage gardens, blowsy plantings, formal European monstrosities."

–Jane Berger, landscape designer and publisher of Garden Design Online

organic and feminine shape serving as counterpoint to square-edged architectural elements. These ancient geometric shapes are both timeless and up-to-the-moment contemporary.

INVEST IN INFRASTRUCTURE Sturdy, hard-working materials like cedar, metal, stone, gravel, and concrete wear through the seasons and the years. If you start out with a flimsy arbor, a raised bed built of wood that will rot, or an uneven terrace, your garden will frustrate you sooner rather than later. And all will need to be replaced all too soon.

If quality materials seem too expensive, realize that cheap ones are more so in terms of both time and cost. Cut back, cut down, but buy quality. Two of the most earth-friendly things you can do are invest in materials that will last and use less of everything. Check out recycled metal and timber. Visit salvage stores, repurpose, reuse. Or develop a smaller area of your property, leaving the rest more naturalistic, so that you can concentrate your efforts and dollars where you'll enjoy them most.

Of course, the more paving (permeable for drainage wherever possible), stepping-stones, and pathways that cover the ground, the less you need to weed. Terraces, patios, and decks lure your family outside to enjoy the garden, as well as provide areas much lower in maintenance than beds or borders. Raised beds, low walls, fences, and hedges divide up space in pleasing ways to provide privacy, enclosure, a sense of intimacy, and separate "garden rooms," all of which give coherence and an edge to the planted areas of the garden.

●

Whether you hire a consultant to visit your garden and lend a fresh eye, have a plan drawn up by a designer or landscape architect, take a class, or read voraciously, your understanding of design will grow and change along with your garden. Some of my favorite books and Web sites to inspire low-maintenance design are listed at the end of this chapter in "Resources."

Take heart in the simple fact that fine design isn't beyond the reach of any of us. It's the result of common sense and having the wisdom to set priorities by figuring out what we really need and want. Clear thinking and clear choices are vital to good design.

This little courtyard garden in Berkeley, California, designed by Shirley Watts, is a lesson in individuality and simplicity. It takes only a few elements to distinguish a garden when they are as strong and distinctive as this supersized arc of aluminum bench, letters embedded in the paving, and an old sign from when the current duplex housed a grocery store.

The generously scaled stone patio and curve of oversized concrete bench in the O'Neill-Soper garden, designed by Cevan Forristt, sets a tone of sturdy comfort and repose.

This heftily scaled wooden dining arbor links indoors and out by extending the architecture and materials of the house out into the garden. Two different varieties of edible grapes clothe the arbor to provide leafy shade and dessert for guests who need only reach to pluck a cluster of dangling grapes.

Designing with low-maintenance in mind takes restraint, the willingness to pare down, elimination of the nonessential. Trust that if you take the time to ask the right questions, you'll find pleasing solutions. A garden, after all, is about the simple pleasures in life like growing fresh food, napping in the sun, tuning in to birdsong and the flit and hover of butterflies and hummingbirds. Gardens should

be a place for kids and dogs to romp, for everyone to relax and take a deep breath of fresh air. And, oh yes, to grow the plants we love best. In our rushed and complicated lives, it's easy to forget that a garden doesn't need to be so complicated.

THE ART IS IN THE EDIT: KATIE EASTON AND TIM FARRELL'S FOLIAGE-CLAD COURTYARD

When twenty-somethings Tim Farrell and Katie Easton bought their first home, a modern "green" townhouse in an urban Seattle neighborhood, their little front courtyard was a mess. Despite their lack of interest in gardening, the couple made the courtyard a priority, for it was the only outdoor space they had besides shared walkways and utility areas.

In a small space, garden design begins by setting priorities. Most of the twelve-by-fourteen-foot Farrell-Easton courtyard is devoted to a table large enough to seat six, for the couple loves to dine and entertain outdoors. They chose bold, easy-care plants to scale up the visuals, such as the fat-leafed *Fatsia japonica* behind Katie, and the bergenia and coleus in containers.

Farrell and Easton, both busy architects and tri-athletes, hadn't time or desire to tend a garden. But they wanted to expand their limited interior space with an inviting view out to the courtyard, as well as relax outdoors and entertain friends al fresco. When every inch counts, as it does in so many urban condos and town-homes, outdoor living space must be as functional and well thought out as a kitchen or bedroom. And with good reason, for outdoor rooms are occupied nearly as many hours a week as interior spaces. In some ways outdoor spaces are even more vital for well-being than inside spaces, because they're used mostly for pleasure and relaxation, high priorities for any urban dweller looking for a little privacy, fresh air, and down time.

This stylish urban courtyard lives larger than its actual diminutive size because of its comfortable table and chairs, simple, sleek pots, and pared-down plant palette.

Tim and Katie's neighbor, Todd Davis, started out with a matching courtyard (below). Todd worked with Junji Miki of Zen Japanese Land-scape Design on a non-plant-centric renovation, paved in stone slabs with a chimenea for evening entertaining.

While the design of the young couple's new townhome focuses on the courtyard, with glass walls on each of three floors, the original view out wasn't too inspiring. The builder had created good bones by paving the space with concrete stepping-stones and enclosing it with a handsome slatted privacy fence with a gate to the side-walk. Oversized glass sliders give easy access from the living room. He didn't do so well when it came to the plants, however, plunking scraggly shrubs into compressed, rubble-filled dirt in a space far too shady for his sun-loving choices. Most of the plants were vigorous growers that would have quickly outstripped the available space and become a pruning nightmare. Easton and Farrell didn't sign off on the punch list until the builder rid the soil of debris and removed every last inappropriate plant, leaving only a coral bark maple (*Acer palmatum* 'Sango-kaku') in one corner.

The advantage of such a small garden is that it doesn't take much money or time to spruce it up and keep it looking good. The challenge is in being selective enough not to clutter and overcrowd the space. These young architects created a successful garden by echoing outside the clean and modern aesthetic of their home. When you start with strong architectural features such as a chartreuse wall, glass sliders, and a concrete floor, all you really need to do is go with the established aesthetic.

They understood scale well enough to know that a small space only looks smaller if the objects in it are dainty. It may seem counterintuitive, but the best way to visually enlarge diminutive spaces is to furnish them with a very few larger pieces. A few sleek and shapely metal pots, a generously scaled wood and metal dining table, and chairs from Design Within Reach so slim they read as silhouettes is all it took to make the space inviting, comfortable, and eminently functional.

But what about plants? Don't they usually come first in a garden? Not in this outdoor room, where replanting what the builder carted away was the last consideration, albeit an important one, for the plants soften and enliven the space. To prevent their plantings from becoming too much work, Easton and Farrell began by making good dirt. They hauled in soil and compost, which wasn't too hard considering it took only a few bags to amend the narrow beds and fill the few pots. These newbie gardeners chose dramatic, easy-care foliage plants for year-round good looks—plants like heuchera, ferns, fatsia, nandina, bergenia, senecio, and phormium, filling in with coleus for summertime color. They chose plants that would thrive in limited sun, wouldn't outgrow the space, and weren't too thirsty.

The results of a weekend or two of effort? An outdoor dining room clothed in foliage, where the couple decompress after work over a glass of wine. An outdoor living room that expands their interior space both visually and actually. And a dining room where they entertain friends and family in every month of the year. Not too bad for a mere 175-square-foot courtyard that looks good and functions well, with no maintenance except the occasional sweeping and watering.

Showy foliage pots lend solidity and stature to this small courtyard garden, providing color and texture in every season. Even old-fashioned, durable perennials like bergenia look fresh and modern in a medley of spiky phormium, colorful heuchera, silvery senecio, and a drip of sedum down the side of a tall metal pot. Such season-stretching foliage pots take little care besides regular summer water.

"I don't apologize for my garden anymore," says Holly Shimizu, a horticulturist, garden writer, television host, and now executive director of the U.S. Botanic Garden. She has a relaxed approach to gardening at home, where she luxuriates in the serene garden retreat designed and cared for with her husband, Osamu.

THE RELAXED GARDEN: HOLLY AND OSAMU SHIMIZU'S TRANQUIL RETREAT

"We aren't fussing over our garden; we're not going for perfection," says U.S. Botanic Garden director Holly Shimizu of her home garden in Glen Echo, Maryland, a tiny, historic town on the Potomac River. Since the mid-1980s, she and her husband, Osamu, a garden designer, have created a sanctuary so charming and atmospheric that people pass by daily to soak up the tranquility emanating through its "neighborhood friendly" fence.

"I love nature, so we try not to overly manipulate our garden," says Holly. "We focus on outdoor living spaces, on making our garden a spiritual oasis with a sense of peacefulness." This avid horticulturist has become far more relaxed about her garden in recent years. "I'm just so glad when a plant likes a certain spot, and is thriving," she says. "The garden has become much shadier over the years as the native paw paw tree and two conifers have grown larger, but there are still plenty of good plants we can grow."

Holly and Osamu have shaped their rectangular garden into a series of loosely linked garden rooms, each with its own distinct feel. While the design may be simple, the impact is powerful. A serene-faced stone Buddha centers the moss garden, a rich tapestry of soft, cushy green. "The only maintenance in the moss garden is trying to keep the squirrels out," says Holly, with a laugh because creatures are welcome in this Certified Backyard Habitat.

The pool garden is a marriage of East and West, with its casual stream and recirculating waterfall plunging into a rectangular swim pool. In years past the pool held a boat and a jungle gym that delighted the couple's kids when they were younger. Now its calm, placid surface reflects the sky.

The terrace garden is the most formal part of the garden, with a patio and series of brick steps, their edges thickly planted in evergreen ground covers. At the foot of the stairs is the meditation garden. A three-tiered fountain provides the sound and beauty of falling water, with ferns, hardy begonias, sweet woodruff, hostas, and native gingers mingling in a restful green plant palette. "This is our little piece of heaven," says Holly of the meditation garden. "It makes me happy. This garden has taught me to appreciate all the shades of green."

Holly's preferred plants are useful as well as beautiful. She loves natives that attract and nurture wildlife: *Lobelia cardinalis* to feed the hummingbirds, the Japanese apricot (*Prunus mume*) for its fragrant winter flowers and the memory it evokes of Osamu's mother shipping from Japan barrels of pickles made from its fruits. "Osamu grew up in Japan," says Holly, "and I've learned from him that foliage and texture are most important. We don't rely on flowers."

Holly sees gardening as our connection to nature and as a source of inspiration, as well as in the larger context of biodiversity. She's careful not to use plants that tend toward invasiveness. "I plant annuals, perennials, shrubs, and trees to encourage pollinators," says Holly, whose diverse, extended-season plantings attract bats, moths, birds, butterflies, and dragonflies. "What life is attracted to my garden? That's the important question."

Brick steps lead down to the lower-level meditation garden, where an invitingly open fence expresses the couple's appreciation for their friendly little town and their love of sharing their garden with neighbors.

A blue bench is the focal point in the terrace garden. Simple design has big impact in this serene garden, where plants are selected for utility, fragrance, and to attract pollinators. "Massing plants to keep down the weeds is the key to low-maintenance," says Osamu.

Between planting so many hardy evergreens, repetition of favorite plants, and simple, clean design, Holly and Osamu have created a garden that's as restful and relaxing for them as for the many passersby who enjoy and take solace from it. "Our garden is joyous to care for, rather than tedious," says Holly. Recently a stranger stopped by to give Holly some apples as a thank you. The woman had been walking by daily since a loved one had died, finding peace and healing in the serene green calm of the Shimizus' garden oasis.

"It's so tempting to junk up gardens with things like gazing globes. We try to make our garden a lesson in restraint," says Holly. It took twenty years for the couple to find this four-foot-tall stone Buddha to anchor their moss garden.

The meditation garden was the first garden room Holly and Osamu designed and planted. The soothing sound of the fountain and the green-on-green plant palette create an atmosphere of peace and tranquility.

"You give kids water to play in and they're happy," says Holly of the recirculating stream, waterfall, and three-foot-deep swim pool that was a magnet for the couple's children and their friends when they were younger. The flagstone edging laced with patterns of pebbles integrates the swim pool into the naturalistic garden.

IT'S NOT ABOUT THE PLANTS: THE NON-PLANT-CENTRIC GARDENS OF CEVAN FORRISTT AND VANESSA KUEMMERLE

The aesthetics and materials used by California garden designers Cevan Forristt and Vanessa Kuemmerle differ widely, yet their gardens have much in common. Each designer creates stylish outdoor living spaces with plants as a small part of the picture.

Their outdoor rooms evoke nature and are open to air and sky yet are as cozy and comfortable as a well-furnished living room. The result is nearly maintenance-free exterior spaces that are a true extension of the house, used by families for relaxing, dining, and entertaining.

It's not that either designer doesn't love plants or isn't well versed in how best to use them. Leafy foliage plants add to the otherworldly feel of Cevan's gardens, and Vanessa abundantly planted the area around the outdoor living room she designed for Chris Bennett in the Saint Francis Wood neighborhood of San Francisco.

The steep garden used to press claustrophobically close to the back of the house. Designer Vanessa Kuemmerle pushed it back with stucco walls to create spacious, gracious outdoor living areas. A trio of glossy urns, each planted with a single succulent, are both easy care and an effective contrast to the rough adobe walls.

The whole idea of exterior rooms may seem more apropos in California, the outdoor-living capital of the country. But no matter our climate, all of us can create equally inviting outdoor spaces, even if we take advantage of them in fewer months of the year. In cold or damp climates, fireplaces, overhead heat lamps, and at least partial cover make outdoor rooms habitable earlier in springtime and longer into autumn.

VANESSA KUEMMERLE Vanessa Kuemmerle says, "I like to keep the flowers to a dull roar, because they just mean more maintenance." Yet lack of flowers is the last thing that comes to mind in the Bennett garden, where Vanessa created sophisticated, inviting outdoor spaces using repurposed materials. She carved the

Ferns and succulents soften the edges of the chimney flue bench, which not only retains the slope but also offers seating. The flues in the top layer function as planter boxes for ornamental grasses and seasonal flowers.

The Bennett back garden is an exercise in restraint, enclosed by eight-foot-tall stucco walls to retain the slope. The furniture is casual and comfortable, the paving outlined in ribbons of cushy blue star creeper.

living spaces out of a steep hillside by retaining the slope with thick stucco walls that shelter an open-air living room. "We pushed the hillside back to give the house a little room to breathe" is how Vanessa describes it.

"In hardscape design, simple is ruling the day," she says. "I use modern materials like concrete and don't hide them." The concrete pavers that floor the Bennett garden are softened by thick ribbons of blue star creeper, the room decorated with pillows and pots.

The contrasting textures and neutral palette of this simple vignette of rough adobe wall and potted conifer evoke a sense of tranquility and repose.

The most arresting feature of the Bennett garden is a repurposed one; a curved bench made of old ceramic chimney flues left over from a remodel of the 1920s-era house. Vanessa planted the top flues with flowers, added cushions and stone steps, and tucked in some sedums around the edges to create an intimate sitting room that's become one of the most popular spots in the garden.

The hillside around the garden has sandy, free-draining soil, so Vanessa planted it thickly in restios and a variety of drought-tolerant South African shrubs well suited to the dry conditions. "The shape, form, and colors of South African plants complement modern aesthetics," says Vanessa, "and they're so easy to care for." Vanessa's designs are based on simple hardscape and governed by planting the right plant in the right place. She sums up her simple, effective design by saying, "It seems undeniable that time has contracted for most people . . . and no one has ever asked me for a high-maintenance garden."

CEVAN FORRISTT Cevan is a red-haired Gemini, a world traveler, and as much of a trip as the award-winning gardens he designs. He plays with space and materials, using oversized elements "to make the spaces sing" and repurposed materials to give an archeological feel to a garden. "My gardens are all about the bones," explains Cevan. "If all the plants died, they'd still look good."

In the O'Neill-Soper garden in Palo Alto, California, Cevan used brawny scale to make the small space feel larger. "You can use less with larger scale . . . you don't need a bunch of dinky crap," says Cevan of the chunky stone pavers and hunky curve of a concrete bench that define the garden. These simple elements are pure quality and strength, the bench linking the garden to the house as it curves toward it, and the russet-toned pavers tying the garden to the earth. "Modern is all about clean lines, the shape, the silhouette. Good design should look great now and a hundred years from now," says Cevan, who describes his style as "earthy yet posh." There's nothing fussy in this garden, just comfort, simple elegance, and a fire pit for the family to gather around as they enjoy being outdoors.

In a larger San Jose garden, Cevan created richly atmospheric garden spaces, inventing a form so new he had to make up a name for it. Thus the "aqua port" was born, a massive cast-concrete keyhole-like structure that collects and directs

"Modern is all about clean lines, shape, silhouette. Good design is a whole new tense that contains the past, present, and future—it looks great now and a hundred years from now."

—Cevan Forristt,
garden designer

With one bold design stroke, Cevan created plentiful seating and a sense of scale. The curve of the brawny bench seems to embrace the house; its length and shape give a feeling of simplicity and intimacy to the entire garden. Yet it's also richly atmospheric, decked out with cushions, candles, and a cozy fire pit.

The open-air buffet, sheltered by the home's roofline, is both useful and an important design element in the O'Neill-Soper garden. The hefty concrete buffet legs, as well as the nearby concrete bench, are embellished with shards of blue-and-white porcelain from dishes broken in a San Francisco earthquake. Such bits and pieces lend a sense of archeology and weathered history to this newly renovated garden.

As classy as a Cevan Forristt garden is, the loose plantings and fun details give it an inviting, casual, lived-in look.

The "aqua port" is both practical and an eye-catching, scale-setting focal point. Water runs down a channel from the aqua port into a raised pond with water lilies.

water into a pond. Cevan put his background in stage sets and ceramics to work when creating this environment unlike any other. "I make my clients their own countries, their own habitats," says Cevan, "It's more like being a site artist than a garden designer." With its twinkling tin lanterns and Asian-inspired furniture, the Holden-Moll garden reflects Cevan's travels to Burma and Indonesia. Despite the garden's exotic feel, the plantings are simple; hardy water lilies float in the pond, while ferns, ornamental grasses, and maples soften the hardscape.

"This garden was designed for entertaining," says Cevan of the various rooms, or "habitats." There's a dining room, a bar area, and a living room, all flowing one

In the Holden-Moll garden, plants form a backdrop for a paved sitting room, with lanterns dangling overhead from the hunky pergola. The blue-and-white pottery encrusting the top of the column is repurposed from ceramics shattered in a San Francisco earthquake.

One of the great charms of a Cevan Forristt garden is that when you pull a chair up to the open-air dining table, you'd be forgiven for a little confusion. Where might you be in the world, and in what era? His designs are both modern and timeless, international with a touch of the Orient.

into the other. Cevan's designs are eco-friendly because they're so timeless and enduring; the gardens are so purely custom, so very personal, that they'll continue to suit and satisfy their owners for many years.

Because hardscape, furniture, fire pits, ponds, and arbors are the stuff of the garden and the plants just the accessories, Cevan's gardens are easy-care and easily habitable through the seasons. "My clients want low maintenance," says Cevan, who puts atmospherics before plants. "I try to capture the past, present, and future in my designs. Maybe I'm creating a whole new tense here, a whole new time warp."

MINIMALISM WITHOUT THE EDGE:
ANITA AND DAVID KAPLAN'S COURTYARD OASIS

An atmosphere of serenity and beauty, as quiet and calming as a gossamer cloak, settles over Anita and David Kaplan's entry courtyard. Materials, plants, and objects have been thoughtfully pared down to the essential few, and the result is a Zen-full space of elegant simplicity. Located high on Seattle's Queen Anne Hill, close to the bustle of the city, the garden is a world apart, timeless in its sense of repose.

The rustle of bamboo and grasses, a rough stretch of driftwood bench, groupings of rustic urns as atmospheric as a gathering of monks all create an aesthetic of minimalism at its best. Nothing is overdone, forced, decorated, or embellished. This is a garden defined by what it doesn't have—no perennials, few flowers, little color, no adornment.

How can such a simple, austere space be so welcoming and satisfyingly sensuous? The design is so spare, the materials so limited, that every detail stands out. Sunshine slants through the slatted screen, and the sweet fragrance of daphne and sarcococca is heady, despite the overall Zen feel of the space.

Enclosed on all sides by fencing, house, and bamboo, the private little garden transcends its location and time. This courtyard could be located anywhere in the world, enhance any style of architecture. Fifty years from now, the Kaplan garden,

A slatted fence and solid metal door lead from the alleyway into this quiet, private oasis of a garden, furnished with a slab of a driftwood bench that serves as both seating and focal point.

designed by landscape architect Randy Allworth of Allworth Nussbaum, will look as coolly modern yet satisfyingly primordial as it does today.

You enter the property from an alleyway, which might be a drawback if the approach weren't so artfully designed. The walkway from alley to courtyard is softened with a phalanx of rustic urns, left unplanted to emphasize their rough texture and sculptural quality. "The urns became part of the architecture of the place," explains Allworth.

Behind the urns, a thick stand of bamboo is skirted with a bed of liriope so lush no weed could pop through. This juxtaposition of the natural and the man-made sets the sophisticated yet simple tone of the garden. Best of all, the courtyard requires no maintenance other than sweeping and a little watering to look as inviting in the dead of winter as in the heat of summer.

The vast view of mountains and boat-busy water is out in front of the house. In back, the courtyard is private, a place apart, where crossing the stone paving to reach the deck and the front door is a chance to put the cares of the world behind you before stepping inside.

Tall, mossy urns pleasantly age the courtyard's interior, their curvy shapes softening the clean lines of the rectilinear space. A fat pot holds a stand of horsetail. A dramatic red-leafed Japanese maple stretches its branches against the backdrop of the concrete wall that shelters the garden from alley passersby. The space is mostly paved in bluestone edged with the cedar decks that lead into the house. Narrow beds are filled with the simplest of plantings—low-growing ribbons of liriope with daphne and sarcococca for fragrance. Rough, monochrome urns in a second grouping are lined up along one side of the space, beating their own ancient rhythm. A driftwood bench provides a sculptural focal point and encourages residents and visitors alike to pause, rest, and soak up the atmospherics.

Why does the space work so well? "The Kaplans are committed to keeping the space simple, clean, and restrained," says Allworth. Then there's the heavy, protective metal entry gate that adds to the courtyard's feel of being its own self-contained world. Yet the space also relates directly to the house. "The garden's materials were chosen with the interiors in mind," says Allworth. Anita shipped the urns home from Thailand, and her love for their rustic good looks inspired the feel of the space. And it was Anita's knowledge of gardening and her desire not to create a maintenance nightmare for herself that led to the courtyard's minimalist, easy-care design. The minute you walk through the gate, you are reminded of how luxurious it can be to have just enough.

PLANTS AS SCULPTURE: LAUREN HALL-BEHRENS'S PORTLAND SANCTUARY

Lauren Hall-Behrens is a Portland, Oregon, garden designer who says of her own home garden, "I wanted a space that's flexible, one I can detail or leave spare. Mostly I don't want to be tied to the garden."

Designer Lauren Hall-Behrens creates low-maintenance gardens for her clients; at home she indulges her love of plants in a stylish garden with a minimalist vibe.

Even before she set out to transform the grassy old orchard behind her turn-of-the-century home into a clean-lined Pan-Asian paradise, Behrens had plenty of experience in designing gardens both beautiful and easy to care for. "The number-one request from all my clients is for low-maintenance," says Behrens. She's most interested in creating spaces that support, nurture, and satisfy her clients, keeping firmly in mind the time and energy it takes to care for the finished product.

Lauren's own aesthetics tend toward modernism. "I'm very drawn to contemporary, minimalist spaces, and I like Asian flair," she says. How to reconcile her desire not to be tied down to maintenance with her love and appreciation for a wide variety of plants? This is the ultimate challenge faced by all of us determined to create more moderate gardens. How do we pare down our plant palette to a

This backyard is an updated orchard; Lauren has pruned up the old fruit trees and planted beneath them, adding a pergola to define the dining terrace.

You know you've arrived somewhere special when you walk up new concrete stairs, past poured-in-place planters, through the stylish metal gate beneath the banana trees and into Lauren's back garden.

Hardscape softened with lush foliage plants defines the contemporary style of Lauren's garden. Gravel, pebbles, and pavers make permeable pathways; the main dining terrace is paved in bluestone.

reasonable size? How can we clothe the bones of the garden in green, plus enrich our gardens with the seasonality plants offer, without turning our gardens into maintenance nightmares?

Few gardeners I've found across the country have solved this basic conundrum as skillfully and gracefully as Lauren has in her Portland backyard. This talented young designer has managed to transform a grassy, aging orchard into as modern a garden as I've seen anywhere, yet it's still rich in the plants Lauren loves best. Her genius lies in creating a space both quiet and dramatic, a restful garden full of plant theatrics, using recycled materials whenever possible.

Her aesthetic is clean and modern, with poured concrete steps and rusty metal touches throughout. Yet to sit in Lauren's garden is as thorough a garden experience as you can imagine, for birds flit and rustle about, lily and rose perfume the air, and the lusciously large-leafed and exotic plants make you think you might be anywhere in the temperate or tropical world.

How did Lauren accomplish such sleight-of-hand? In answer to that question, she shared a few of her best tips and techniques for plant-rich, low-maintenance gardening with me. "I think of plants as sculpture, choosing them for their

Lauren's garden relies on architectural elements to set the cool, contemporary tone. A casual gravel-and-paver pathway leads to the garden's new portal, a stunning metal gate set into a pergola painted to match the house. Bear's breech (*Acanthus mollis*) flowers to the right of the path; to the left are tufts of bleached blonde Mexican feather grass (*Stipa tenuissima*).

forms as well as textures. When you don't want to overpopulate your garden with hard-to-care-for plants, this concept will help you choose plants that deliver the most drama and structure possible."

Effective editing means choosing, and sticking with, the plants you love most. "I use plants for their personalities," says Lauren. "Like that rose (*Rosa mutabilis* 'Bengal Fire')—its color is 'Stare At Me!'" In this most modern of gardens, Lauren also grows plenty of old-fashioned favorite plants like hydrangeas, roses, and lilies.

Lauren pays attention to the big picture of creating atmosphere with privacy fencing and a canopy of banana trees beneath the old fruit trees, as well as the details. Luminous little cairns of glass slag draw your eyes down to appreciate the smaller plant treasures, while overhead colorful sedums drip from metal grate-like pots hanging from tree limbs.

Lauren starts her designs with year-round structures and forms, like evergreens for screening, walls, and fences. She masses slim upright evergreens like winter-blooming, vanilla-scented boxleaf azara (*Azara microphylla*), *Cupressus* 'Tiny Tower', or *Euonymus* 'Green Spire' to create screening and privacy. Metal edging keeps beds tidy while raising the grade of the soil for better drainage.

Lauren uses plants for structure and punctuation to create drama, but she also repeats plants over and over for ease of care. She masses her favorite plants, and she repeats them in various spots throughout the garden to create visual unity. Dozens of pale 'Milky Way' lungworts (*Pulmonaria*) encircle the gravel terrace, fluffs of bleached blonde Mexican feather grass (*Stipa tenuissima*) line paths, while dark-leafed heucheras, golden Japanese forest grass, and strawberries trim the beds.

Lauren keeps down weeds and fluffs up the garden by massing ground covers, overlapping them for textural effect. She grows spidery black mondo sprouting out of golden *Sedum makinoi* 'Ogon'. For contrast, or in areas where it's hard to get ground covers to thrive, she uses sweeps of Mexican pebbles or blankets of black Japanese stones to cover the ground.

Flowers are Lauren's last consideration when choosing plants. Structure and foliage come first, resulting in a plant palette that is all about form and texture, with pops of seasonal bloom. She relies on fountains of ornamental grasses, fat-leafed plants like lungwort and bananas, and stalwart evergreens to carry the garden through the seasons.

Although the garden feels lush and near-tropical, much of it is hardscaped. Poured concrete stairs, planters, and patios, pebble and stone walkways, and a gravel terrace make the garden handsome and easily navigable, and cut way down on maintenance.

Despite the concrete, rusty metal fencing, and metal-edged beds, this garden is all about comfort for both people and plants. The scale is intimate, and the chairs (from Ikea) are so deep you never want to get up. There are plenty of spaces to rest your eye as well as yourself. Plants thrive in the well-amended soil, and each looks well nurtured. And yet this garden's success relies on Lauren's ability to consider both people and plants in her design. She's reached a happy compromise between plant possibility and human resources of time, money, and energy.

"It's so important to have a beginner's eye when designing gardens," says Lauren. "It's too easy to get lost in the work and lose the joy, the lightness of mind and attitude." Lauren has practiced this joyful attitude in designing her own garden, with the result that "I sit and look around, watch the light change, and see so many things that please me." "It feels so good to be out here," Lauren concludes.

" It's modern to use plants in a playful way, almost as an artistic medium to create atmospheres and spaces—that's what resonates with me. Spaces that are conceptual—I'd say that's modern."

–Lauren Hall-Behrens, garden designer

A metal fence lends privacy to a serene little gravel terrace, outlined in *Pulmonaria* 'Milky Way' backed by slim little 'Tiny Tower' cypress. Such simple, repetitive planting creates a calm, quiet atmosphere, emphasizes the garden's geometry, and is a breeze to care for.

SKY-HIGH SUSTAINABILITY: GREG SMITH'S
SLEEK WRAPAROUND DECK GARDEN

Twelve stories up in a condo tower in downtown Seattle, Greg Smith's wraparound deck is sleekly modern, comfortably inviting, and designed to be as maintenance-free as any garden containing plants could ever hope to be.

"Greg doesn't want to tinker in the garden, but he was interested in how the space felt," says landscape architect Dale Nussbaum of Allworth Nussbaum. "And

Masses of dwarf maiden grass (*Miscanthus sinensis* 'Yaku Jima') soften the view out to the city. All the color and pattern in the garden come from the furniture, pots, and accessories, for the plant palette is tough, durable, and year-round green.

he wanted the garden to be as sustainable as possible." Modern, edgy, and organic might not seem compatible adjectives, but all apply. The garden is constructed of renewable ipe (pronounced e-pay) wood and local stone along with galvanized steel, durable choices as handsome as they are long-lasting.

The garden's furniture, pots, and planters appear stout, sturdy, and rooted to the ground (well, the deck), but in fact the elements are "floating" on Styrofoam and pedestals. "It's all highly calculated and engineered for weight," explains Nussbaum. And yet the garden has weathered windstorms and regularly endures blazing sun and harsh winds, all part of the highly dynamic conditions way up there in the sky.

Plant selection was exacting—What plants can survive container life, battered by sun, glare, and wind, with minimal care? Keep in mind that on three sides of the condo, a spectacular tapestry of water, mountains, and city stretches out behind the plants, so each must look great year-round so as not to distract from that many-million-dollar view.

To this end, Nussbaum repeated a tough, textural palette of ornamental grasses, sedum, and bamboo. A thick stand of golden bamboo screens the bathroom, so the view out from the soaking tub is through leafy green to the lights and towers of the city beyond. Pines, maples, and native evergreens like Pacific

The expansive deck surface is floored in unfinished ipe wood, concrete pavers and local stone pebbles. The dining table is sheltered by a stand of bamboo growing in galvanized steel containers.

A voluptuously alluring, built-in double reclining chaise invites you to relax and enjoy the view, twelve stories up on Greg Smith's deck. This garden is as well furnished as most interiors, but the plants and construction materials are sustainable, low-maintenance, and durable enough to hold up under the punishing conditions so high in the sky.

Feather reed grass 'Karl Foerster' is planted amidst a sea of sedums. Interspersed containers create a dramatic yet easy-care, year-round foliage display that plays off the clean, spare lines of this ultra-urbanist garden.

A simple slatted wooden screen hung with sedum-filled metal boxes makes an effective, low-maintenance, living screen.

wax myrtle (*Myrica californica*) fill the galvanized steel containers and ceramic pots, all plants that need nothing but a little water to stand full and sturdy in every season of the year. Their rough good looks contrast pleasingly with the sleek custom-made fire table and a reclining double chaise so seductively soft and comfy that it beckons you in for a nap. The plants are rock-bottom durable, the furniture coolly contemporary, and it all works.

Perhaps the ultimate low-maintenance element is the living sedum screen that divides the deck's public spaces from the more intimately scaled private spaces. Built of ipe wood, the screen sports a modernist interpretation of window boxes. Drought-tolerant sedums fill rows of galvanized steel planters lined up all along the face of the screen, creating a neo–hanging-garden-of-Babylon that does its job of screening off the private part of the deck outside of the bathrooms and bedrooms.

Elegant, sleek, and modern are what we might expect from a high-rise condo deck garden. Designed to suit Greg Smith's busy schedule, interests, and ethics, the garden is also sustainable, organic, and nearly maintenance-free.

LOW-MAINTENANCE GARDENS THAT DON'T LOOK IT

When you see stylish, luscious, functional, plant-rich gardens like those of Katie Easton and Tim Farrell, Lauren Hall-Behrens, and Greg Smith, or those designed by Cevan Forristt or Vanessa Kuemmerle, low-maintenance is the last thing that comes to mind. Thoughtful, well-designed low-maintenance gardens don't look it, in part because they're as varied as their topography and climate, and each reflects the needs and aesthetics of the gardener who tends it.

Despite differences in style, size, cost, and location, these new low-maintenance gardens have certain characteristics in common:

- **Simplicity.** The underlying design is strong and simple, at a comfortably large scale. Adornment and embellishment, in most cases, is kept to a minimum. The complications are left to the plants, which by their very nature as living things are complex, multilayered, and ever-changing.
- **Repetition.** Too much variety, in either plants or materials, creates a maintenance nightmare. In well-designed gardens, materials are repeated in a variety of ways, and favorite, successful plants are massed or used again and again in pots, beds, and borders. Such repetition creates a pleasing rhythm, rests the eye, and makes gardens easier to care for.
- **Personality.** The joy of these gardens lies in their compelling individuality, for each is a reflection of the gardener and of the family that occupies it.
- **Thoughtful and stringent editing.** These gardens have a certain coherence to them—they make visual sense—because the hard choices to eliminate the extraneous have been made. These gardens are pared down to the functional and the beautiful, so that each plant, piece of artwork or furniture, and architectural element is made the most of. While less is definitely more when it comes to maintenance, easy-care gardens aren't single-note, austere, or plant-bereft spaces, as you can see from the stunning gardens profiled in this chapter.
- **Friendliness to the earth.** A healthy garden starts from the soil up with organics, smart plant choices, and considerations of regional materials and native plants, and it thrives with less intervention from the gardener.

Mitchell Smith and Evette Gee in their garden, which is as comfortably furnished and thoroughly accessorized as any other room in the house. The couple visited twenty-three countries in a year, bringing back a wealth of treasures to deck out their garden.

PLANTS IN THE SUPPORTING ROLE: MITCHELL SMITH AND EVETTE GEE'S EXOTIC OUTDOOR WORLD

Mitchell Smith and Evette Gee are a cosmopolitan couple who crafted an outdoor environment as worldly as they are. Plants aren't the point in this Seattle garden, for they simply play the role of backdrop and canopy in a series of outdoor rooms that can serve as a quiet sanctuary or a place for partying. The garden floor is mostly lawn or pavement and is often strewn with Turkish carpets; overhead, starry lanterns dangle from tree limbs. The result is an open-air stage set of a garden that could be located almost anywhere in the world.

Evette and Mitchell left corporate jobs to travel the world, visiting twenty-three different countries in a year. Along the way they collected not only memories but also stone Buddhas, furniture, and an entire joglo (open-air room) from Java, all of which they shipped home to adorn their garden.

With hard work and an eye for exotic artifacts, the pair has transformed their city lot into a garden that's all about décor and atmospherics. It's unapologetically not about the plants. "I plant what I like visually," says Mitchell. "I don't know the names. And I've given up on grass—I just put in more moss."

The joglo is the centerpiece of the garden, built over the koi pond. In Java, joglos are sacred ceremonial spaces for marriages and births.

The couple made sure the exterior infrastructure was in place before setting in to decorate the garden. Mitchell, an architect with an eye for scale and proportion if not so much for plants, wrapped the property in tall wooden fences for privacy and installed a sprinkler system that irrigates every corner. Overhead, a canopy of timber bamboo, cherry trees, and maples pretty much roofs the entire back garden in leafy shade. Feeding the koi, lighting the candles, and sweeping the walkways is pretty much the extent of the work needed to keep the garden spruced up. A leaf blower, a broom, and a pair of long-handled pruners are all the tools needed to keep these outdoor rooms livable.

Just off the kitchen is the new outdoor dining room, lit at night by lanterns and floating candles for an aura of tranquil privacy. The arbor, with slatted ceiling and wooden walls and paving underfoot, makes this outdoor space habitable year-round.

One of the many buddhas that populate the garden. The statuary creates a serene atmosphere as well as lending year-round presence and structure. In that way it's not unlike a shrub, but buddhas don't grow or need pruning, watering, and fertilizing.

Both Evette and Mitchell were greatly influenced by the centuries-old gardens they visited in Japan and Indonesia, and by cultures and climates where people live outdoors much of year. "We loved how minimalist the gardens were, how serene, the spirituality of it all," says Evette.

What was once a narrow side yard has been refashioned into an intimate dining area framed with handsome arbor, gate, and fencing. A long dining table sits alongside the pond and rushing waterfall Smith built as tribute to the couple's trip to Africa's Victoria Falls. Stroll through the carved gateway to find a promenade of Buddha statues practicing their lotus positions, then into a lantern-bedecked, fern-rich back garden. Follow the path to the fully furnished joglo built over a koi pond. This open-air room seems to float above the water, its intricately carved wooden ceiling speaking of other times and cultures. Continue around the house to the party spot the couple calls the "opium den" with its Moroccan vibe of cushions and patterned carpet. "You could be anywhere in the world out here in the garden," says Evette, as a finch lands on a nearby Buddha and the bamboo rustles overhead.

NO-STRESS SUCCULENTS: JEONG HYEON LEE'S STURDY YET EXOTIC DESIGNS

Succulents are the plants of the future. They define diversity with their wide array of colors, textures, and shapes. Climate change? Succulents are adaptable. Drought? They prefer arid conditions. What clinches their status as the "it" plants of today and tomorrow is succulents' uncanny ability to practically take care of themselves.

Using her own succulent-rich urban plot as a model of easy-care, environmentally savvy gardening, San Francisco designer Jeong Hyeon Lee recommends her favorite plants to all her clients. "Succulents are the opposite of perennials," she says. "They do best if you don't pay too much attention to them."

Are her clients persuaded to give up their perennial borders and hydrangeas? "At first they think of cactus and don't want spiny, sharp plants. But when they see how varied succulents are and how easy to care for, they love them."

Jeong's own tiny garden in the Bernal Heights neighborhood of San Francisco is packed with the weird and wonderful textural undulations of sedums, aloes, echeveria, agaves, and aeoniums. Most are frost hardy, some are more tropical, many could survive outdoors in most areas of the country. The diversity is vast, the colors exciting, and the showy flowers a bonus, for Jeong plants for shape and texture rather than bloom.

While they don't need watering, dividing, or fertilizing, succulents do require perfect drainage, which is hard to achieve in a perfectly flat garden. Jeong builds up two-foot mounds of soil, retained by short rock walls, in which to plant. If soil is heavy or clay-filled, as in her own garden, she mixes in pumice and lava rock to lighten it up and improve drainage. "Succulents, even the less hardy ones, can take brief cold spells, but they can't tolerate wet feet," she advises.

The varied hardscape and dramatic succulents are contemporary yet timeless enough to complement Jeong Lee's late-nineteenth-century house in San Francisco. The chocolate-colored *Aeonium arboreum* 'Zwartkop' is in the foreground, with a clump of *Aloe striata* across the path. The blue-green fleshy leaves are *Agave celsii* var. *albicans*.

"Succulents are modern; they make you focus on shapes, patterns, and lines."

–Jeong Hyeon Lee, garden designer

Aeoniums and agaves thrive in a windy oceanfront garden; the shrub in the background is a pittosporum and the tree a Monterey cypress, both good succulent companions because they're equally drought tolerant. Designer Jeong Lee built up the beds in Thomas Lloyd-Butler's garden with low rock walls to show off the succulents to best advantage and to give them better drainage.

MAKE SUCCULENTS THE STARS IN YOUR GARDEN

Here's Jeong Lee's expert advice on making succulents the stars in your garden:

- Give succulents perfect drainage by amending the soil with lava rock and pumice, and building up planting beds a foot or two. They're easy to propagate, easy to transplant. Succulents are patient—you can dig them up and let them sit there for a month until you have time to get back to them.

- The less you fuss, the better succulents perform. The drier the garden, the more intense the color; succulents that are starved of water turn brilliant shades. They also grow more compact when you don't fertilize or overwater. How do you know when to water? The plants will tell you: when they get a little dessicated looking, a little wrinkled, it's time to give them a drink.

- To find the best succulents for your climate, contact your local or regional cactus and succulent society and attend their sales. Jeong Lee also recommends Yucca Do Nursery in Texas as a dependable source of interesting succulents, including many hardy ones (www.yuccado.com).

- A couple of beauties to try in colder climates include *Manfreda* 'Macha Mocha' (a.k.a. *Agave* 'Macha Mocha'), which can take temperatures down to 9 degrees F; artichoke look-alike *Agave parryi* and *Yucca rostrata*, which are both hardy; plus all the different sempervivums, which look tropical but aren't.

- When you design with succulents, think of them as having the same virtues as a black-and-white photo. You aren't distracted by color so can take advantage of their strong shapes, lines, and forms.

"It's gorgeous!" declares succulent worshiper Jeong Lee of the purple-toned *Agave* 'Macha Mocha'. Introduced by Yucca Do Nursery in Texas, this beauty is hardy down to a surprising 9 degrees F. The silvery fingerlike plant is *Cotyledon orbiculata*, and in the background is the large, strappy-leaved *Agave Americana*.

Good companions for succulents include other drought-tolerant plants with contrasting shapes and textures, like conifers and broadleaf evergreens. Jeong mixes a few equally low-maintenance phormiums, pittosporums, and Monterey cypress into her landscapes to introduce height and varying forms that show off the rosette, spiky, and mounding shapes of the succulents.

Whenever Jeong is confronted with a tough site, succulents are her solution. The front garden she designed for Thomas Lloyd-Butler is now such a lush extravaganza of sedum, you wouldn't guess this beachfront property is windy, foggy, and frequently sprayed with salt water. Jeong left the Monterey cypress to frame the house, building up beds a foot or so to best show off the agaves, aeoniums, and aloes that thrive despite the difficult conditions.

Jeong tells the story of an eighty-year-old client who came to her wanting to cut down on water usage. The client was used to her lawn and hydrangeas but was open to trying something new. "We ripped out all the lawn and replaced it with succulents," says Jeong. "She loves her new garden . . . bless her heart."

Keep It Simple

- Design isn't just to look at—it's the ultimate maintenance tool. A strong design, well planned and executed, reduces maintenance more than any other factor. Whether you prefer geometry in the form of circles, squares, and rectangles, or more naturalistic curves, be sure to establish your garden's design before planting. The more thought you put into the design, the better your garden will look through the seasons with less involvement from you.

- Plant succulents. These drought-tolerant uber-plants for the new millennium are architecturally shaped, stunning in their variety, easy to transplant and propagate, hardier than you'd expect if you give them good drainage, and once established, like Greta Garbo, prefer to be left alone. San Francisco designer Jeong Lee calls succulents "adaptable, diverse, no-stress plants."

- Take advantage of plant structure and form to bring height, punctuation, and drama to the garden. Think shape and size first, with flowers as a last consideration, to create an easy-care garden that keeps its good looks through the seasons. Choose hardy, reliable evergreens with interesting shapes to form the backbone of your plantings. In summertime, lush annual vines grown up screens or trellises add near-instant privacy, texture, and color, as do perennials chosen for their structure or voluptuousness, such as cardoons, dahlias, ligularia, and gunnera.

- When a garden is spare rather than overcrowded, every detail stands out to full

"I wish people would give up the notion of garden equals flowers. Flowers are a transient bonus; you don't have to wait for flowers to enjoy your garden."

–Jeong Hyeon Lee, garden designer

advantage. This is the luxury of enough, when each well-selected or favorite item in your garden is made the most of. A beautifully pruned specimen tree, a single urn, a sculptural bench or vividly colored umbrella when singled out and treated as a piece of art can have great impact. The result? Less to care for in a garden that is every bit as satisfying as, if not more satisfying than, one that is overpacked with plants and décor.

- Materials and objects that do double duty cut down on maintenance. If you decide on an undrilled container for a water garden, grow a tall papyrus during the summer or horsetails year-round to add near-instant height and an exotic feel to the garden. A sculptural bench can serve as a focal point as well as a place to sit. Paving can be patterned or colored to liven up or texturize the garden while doing its job of providing a hard, dry surface to walk on (see the Kaplan garden for examples of all these double-duty tricks). Perhaps the ultimate double-duty paving is pebble mosaics, which introduce craftsmanship, color, and pattern into the garden while offering a foot reflexology treatment every time you walk across them.

Gillian Matthews crafted several small pebble mosaics in her urban garden to introduce pattern and texture at ground level.

- Turn design challenges into assets. On a difficult site with a streambed in the front garden, Bethesda, Maryland, designer Melissa Clark transformed the soggy area into a design feature. She lined the streambed with river rock to create a gracious curving line through the front garden. She planted the sides of the streambed with plants that can adapt to the changing water table, like native sweet spire (*Itea virginica*) for its bronze fall foliage, shrubby dogwoods, and 'Karl Foerster' feather reed grass. Alliums planted higher up on the banks lend spring color, and hostas lush up the scene in summer.

Melissa Clark's design turned a soggy area into a design feature in this Bethesda, Maryland, front garden.

- Editing—or what you might prefer to think of as choosing to give garden room only to what you love most—is the most essential low-maintenance discipline a gardener can learn. As you design your garden spaces, think about how you most use the garden. Dedicate space to eating outdoors, napping, and reading with comfortable, sturdy furniture. Then consider the shapes, materials, and plants you love most. If you stick to the circle shapes that satisfy you, that tawny color of stone or gravel that warms your heart, or the one quintessential rose or hydrangea, you won't feel deprived, and your garden won't be crowded or labor-intensive.

- A single strong design concept unifies a garden, makes it comprehensible and restful to the eyes and the soul. This means fewer plants and accessories are needed, for the garden stands on its own without much embellishment. In my own garden, this meant sticking to a restricted color palette. In the Kaplan garden, every component conspires to create the Zenlike atmosphere that permeates the space. In the multicultural garden of Mitchell Smith and Evette Gee, collected objects artfully blur the geographic and climatic boundaries between the temperate and tropical world. In every case, the result is a low-maintenance garden that doesn't look it.

- Repetition. Let me repeat that—repetition, repetition. The most design-savvy, easy-care gardens make use of the same materials, embellishments, and plants again and again to create rhythm, unify the garden, and make the whole so much easier to care for. In Greg Smith's rooftop garden, unfinished ipe wood is used for flooring and screens. Rows of rustic urns set the tone and beat a pleasing rhythm in Anita Kaplan's garden. Discovering which plants do well in your garden and then repeating them in different combinations and situations is a sure way to make a garden that's as easy to care for as it is aesthetically pleasing.

Resources

BOOKS The books listed here are available in libraries, online, and in used book shops if they're no longer in print. Many aren't exactly geared to simplifying your gardening life—in fact, quite the opposite, for they're full of ideas, inspiration, and temptingly beautiful items and plants. Yet each is also rich in style, flair, and wisdom that will help you examine your preferences, memories, needs, and aesthetics, a vital step on the way to crafting your own satisfying, personal, and simplified garden. They offer a window on design around the world, with fresh ideas to stir us up and expand our minds to all that gardens can be.

Architecture in the Garden by James van Sweden (Random House, 2002). A stylebook of materials and a lesson in scale; the schematic drawings in this book, paired with the many photos, are an easily absorbed lesson in garden design.

Artists in Their Gardens by Valerie Easton and David Laskin (Sasquatch Books, 2001). Writing this book helped me to understand gardens on a much

Ornamental grasses, maples, pines, and arbutus in pots frame the ingenious sedum screen that divides the public parts of the deck from the more private ones. Newly planted sedums will eventually spill down the fronts of the containers arrayed on the screen, designed as a modernist interpretation of old-fashioned window boxes.

deeper level than the visual, for artists design gardens from their hearts and their guts. Take a trip through the very personal gardens of ten visual artists who shape space and create atmospherics, using plants as just one of their many mediums.

Avant Gardeners: 50 Visionaries of the Contemporary Landscape by Tim Richardson (Thames and Hudson, 2008). With its international perspective, uber-cool aesthetics, and emphasis on the conceptual, this photo-laden tribute to modernity expands our minds to all the possibilities of visual landscapes (you can't really quite call many of them gardens).

Color by Design: Planting the Contemporary Garden by Nori and Sandra Pope (Soma Books, 1998). The bible of color gardening, a gorgeous book full of the history, love, and mystery of color, as well as practical advice on shades, tints, and combinations. I read this book again and again, especially in winter when I'm color- and flower-deprived.

The Complete Pebble Mosaic Handbook by Maggy Howarth (Firefly Books, 2003). Ancient Chinese pebble mosaics look as fresh and modern today as they did centuries ago, in this authoritative book that manages to be practical and instructive as well as an inspiring style manual.

Gardens of a Golden Afternoon by Jane Brown (Van Nostrand Reinhold, 1982). I've read this book cover to cover at least three times for its lovely evocation of a lost time and place, and the author's insight into Gertrude Jekyll's gardens and Edward Lutyen's architecture and how the two intersected so triumphantly. If you, too, find Jekyll's own writings impenetrable, this book will translate Jekyll-speak so you can enjoy her genius.

New Garden Design: Inspiring Private Paradises by Zahid Sardar (Gibbs Smith, 2008). This stunning book is garden porn, filled with oversized images of mostly California gardens. But if you look closely enough to deconstruct many of the gardens, there are low-maintenance lessons to be learned amidst the grandeur, in the use of art, unexpected materials, and the personalized, modernist aesthetic.

Outdoors: The Garden Design Book for the Twenty-First Century by Diarmuid Gavin and Terence Conran (Octopus Ltd., 2007). Designer and restaurateur Conran teamed up with the avant-garde Dublin designer Gavin to produce a book that redefines oversize and makes you realize every garden book should have photos this huge. You feel as if you step right into these glorious photos of global gardens. Not just an extravaganza of cool materials and offbeat design, many of these gardens feature spaces for outdoor living and vegetables and demonstrate a conservation ethic for the new millennium. Mogul Conran was clever to enlist contemporary designer and garden personality Gavin to up the cool quotient on this visually inspiring idea book.

A Pattern Garden: The Essential Elements of Garden Making by Valerie Easton (Timber Press, 2007). Inspired by Christopher Alexander's book *A Pattern Language*, I've tried to bring the language of patterns to gardeners, giving them the confidence and tools to design enchanting, personal, and emotionally fulfilling outdoor spaces, with the visuals missing in Alexander's black-and-white tome.

A Pattern Language: Towns, Buildings, Construction by Christopher Alexander (Oxford University Press, 1977). Architect Alexander says that people not only can but should design their own spaces and has distilled some 250 "patterns" that affect the way we live, stir our emotions, and create satisfying rooms, indoors and out. More than thirty years after it was first published, Alexander's book is still in print.

The Small Garden by John Brookes (Marshall Cavendish, 1982); *The Essentials of Garden Design* by John Brookes (Knopf, 2008). No one explains the underlying geometry of good gardens as well as John Brookes. *The Small Garden* is the first book that enlightened me to the fact that gardens are more than a conglomeration of plants. Brookes has explored this theme in photos, clear text, and drawings in every book since; be sure to have at least one on your bookshelf.

The Tiny Garden by Jane McMorland Hunter (Frances Lincoln, 2006). This is a stylish book filled with clever little gardens that live far bigger than their footprint. Those who garden in passageways and courtyards, on balconies and decks, and in any corner they can find can take heart in the fact there's nothing atmospherically small about these comfy, colorful garden spaces.

ONLINE RESOURCES **Garden Design Online**, www.gardendesignonline.com. The brainchild of Washington, DC, journalist and garden designer Jane Berger, this site keeps you up to date on books, gardens to visit, and what's going on around the world in garden design. Does Jane travel constantly so we don't have to? Check out the especially useful "hot and cool links" to find the best on the net in blogs and Web pages on garden design.

A pittosporum shrub above a border of agaves and senecios withstands all the drought, wind, and salt spray this Jeong Lee beachside garden is subject to.

Make It Work

OUR GARDENING METHODS AND ROUTINES can save every bit as much time, labor, and money as thoughtful design and plant choice. Much of the advice in this chapter is nothing more than putting good, old-fashioned organic gardening principles into practice. Why not piggyback onto what good gardeners have learned over the years?

Tips, Tricks, and Strategies for Simplifying Garden Work

Let's face it—gardening isn't all that efficient. Nature is messy, weather happens, plants grow (or die) in ways we never expect or intend. Gardening can feel a bit aimless as we roam from one project to another, experiment, get great ideas, get tired out. This creative dance with our gardens is a pleasure, but sometimes we want to finish up certain tasks and move on to the fun part. These tips and tricks will help:

- **Keep an autumn sensibility.** The most effective strategy of all is to embrace the living, ever-changing, organic nature of a garden, and to see those qualities

ABOVE: Water features need not be big and noisy to exude atmospherics. In artist Ted Hoppin's Bainbridge Island garden, a simple stove basin holds water to reflect the sky.

OPPOSITE: An island garden of edibles and ornamentals was renovated for easier care. Raised beds of poured concrete, sturdy trellises, artful focal points like the line of glass cloches, and a thick layer of mulch to keep down weeds make the garden easier to tend and keep it looking tidy and attractive through the seasons.

as great joys rather than something to try and control. Be grateful for the plants that are thriving in your garden and revel in nature's surprises. You'll not only enjoy your garden more, but I promise you that you'll also find your relaxed garden to be a more attractive and welcoming one.

Think of it as keeping an autumn sensibility year-round. You know how in October, when the leaves fall and plants decline, it's easier to appreciate the beauty of change? Somehow in autumn we're able to accept the garden as just what it is. A little of that sensibility spread throughout the gardening year helps to temper our springtime eagerness and our summer perfectionism. U.S. Botanic Garden Executive Director Holly Shimizu says it best: "My dream is for the perception of our gardens to change enough to accept imperfections." Blur your eyes a bit and accept messiness as part of the pleasure of gardening.

- **Put plants where they want to grow.** You'll find there are plenty of rewarding plants for nearly every gardening condition. Take your cue from the plants themselves so you don't engage in a battle you'll never win. Put plants where they want to grow, with companions that suit them.

- **Repeat what works.** Repeating what works is a good design strategy and an even greater low-maintenance one. You'll know you've planted the right ground cover in the right place when you notice it happily spreading about, or the right tree or shrub when it's bursting with health and vigor. So divide, propagate, or buy more of them. Repeating plants lends coherence and harmony to a garden while making it easier to care for.

- **Research eventual plant size before purchase.** Every cute little plant in a nursery pot looks innocent, and I'm sorry to say you should take the eventual height and girth given on the tag as no more than a suggestion. Visualizing scale is very tricky; it's difficult to picture thirty feet high and wide when considering a little green nubbin. And besides, we gardeners tend to fall in love and delude ourselves about any plant's growth potential.

Especially when it comes to trees and shrubs, read up on eventual size before purchase. Check out local publications that describe how plants do in your climate and consult books like *The Illustrated Encyclopedia of Trees* by David More, which shows a tree's profile and spread over time. Better yet, visit local botanical gardens and arboreta to see mature specimens of any tree or larger shrub you're considering letting loose in your garden. Many a gardener has been frustrated by a shrub grown into a tree, or a garden ruined by the dank, dark shade cast by a tree grown far larger than ever imagined. So save yourself trouble, time, and money (tree pruning and removal is expensive) by buying woody plants well suited to the space you have to give them.

- **Garden with the seasons.** Garden with the rhythm of the seasons, not against them. Starting in autumn, use bulb planting as a cue. It's time to cut down enough of the dying foliage in your garden to give easy access to the soil to bury the bulbs. Then in early spring, finish up the cleaning so you can prepare the soil for summer. Dig in any fertilizer you plan to apply, top-dress with compost, then layer mulch on top, and your garden is cleaned up and ready for spring growth and summer drought. Pay attention to the changes in your plants, weather, and temperature to determine routines in sync with your own particular garden and climate.

- **See rain as your friend.** Rain is your friend for more reasons than just watering the plants. Always weed after it rains, for it's much easier to dislodge and pull roots when the ground is thoroughly soaked. Fertilize when it's raining or rain is predicted, so fertilizer will be gently and thoroughly watered in by nature rather than by blasts from the hose.

- **Dig the perfect planting hole.** Get plants off to the best start possible by digging the perfect planting hole. No matter what kind of plant, the hole you dig should look like a shallow bowl, as deep as the plant's root system and twice as wide. Then backfill with the native soil you dug out of the hole, gently firm with your hands, water in well, and mulch around the plant's root zone.

- **Irrigate until plants are established.** Remember that every plant, no matter how drought tolerant, needs regular irrigation the first couple of years until its roots are extensive enough that it can fend for itself during the drier times of the year.

- **Transplant in cool, damp weather.** It's possible to plant and transplant almost any time when the ground isn't frozen, but you'll be much more successful with these chores when the weather is cool and damp. This is true whether you're planting tiny starts of flowers or vegetables in springtime, potting up

> "For me, garden is a verb, not a noun. It's the act of going outside and connecting with the plant kingdom."
>
> –Amy Stewart, author

plants from the nursery, or struggling to move a big rhododendron you originally planted in the wrong spot. No plant likes its roots exposed to sun, heat, and dry air, so wait for drizzle and cloud cover.

- **Follow basic garden hygiene and safety rules.** Sharpen your tools so you don't rip or shred plants, and clean them regularly so you don't spread disease. Wear boots and gloves so you don't hurt yourself. Use your tools for their intended purposes. Get help when something is too heavy for you to lift or move by yourself. Wear a hat, long pants, and long sleeves except on the hottest days to protect yourself from sun, weather, thorns, and general garden muck and mess. Put all perennial weeds in a sealed bag and toss into the garbage, not into your compost pile.

- **Dispose of unsuccessful plants pronto.** Don't waste any time, angst, or garden space nursing along plants that are diseased or generally struggling. There are too many good plants to waste your time this way, plus fighting a losing battle with your plants makes you feel like a bad gardener. Why not court success by composting or otherwise disposing of unsuccessful plants and starting over with plants that will thrive in your garden?

- **Always use a tarp when cleaning up the garden.** Using a tarp will save you literally hours of time and much frustration. If you throw clippings and weeds onto paths, gravel, and lawn, you make even more of a mess than you started with. Who wants to spend time cleaning up after themselves more than they have to? Drag a tarp around your garden, cover up the ground before you start working, toss your mess onto the tarp. It's that easy. So do it. Every time.

- **Favor simple, natural, and nontoxic.** Simple, natural, nontoxic products can be effective and inexpensive in the garden. For example, alfalfa meal pushes bloom in roses, dahlias, clematis, and other flowering plants. Work a couple of cups into the ground around the base of shrubs, less for perennials, and water in well. To kill weeds, pour boiling water right out of the teakettle or spray full-strength white vinegar from the grocery store, applying several times. (Be warned, vinegar will kill any plant it hits, not just the weeds). To give plants a boost, mix Epsom salt with water and apply at planting (for details, see www.epsomsaltcouncil.org). Epsom salt contains magnesium, which helps seeds germinate and nourishes plants.

- **Slow down out there.** This is the second best strategy of all—slow down out there in your garden. Look closely at your plants as you tend them, breathe in their sweet and spicy scents, stroke their leaves, feel the breeze, listen to the birds. Soak up all the beauty and mystery in your garden while you work. As you tune in to all the life going on around you while caring for your garden, you'll grow your own health, tranquility, and sense of wonder.

Cover the Ground

At its most basic, gardening comes down to covering the ground. Outside our doors lies bare earth with potential. How we use that potential is up to us, and the myriad of possibilities ensures that gardeners are the least bored people on the planet.

What we don't ever want to do is leave a void for weeds to take over, or create an eco-nightmare by paving over too much of our property. Between these two extremes, there are plenty of earth-friendly, low-maintenance choices.

A waterfront garden is paved with bluestone to create a dining terrace and seating area amid masses of low-growing drought-tolerant perennials. The effect is serene, and the landscape low-maintenance.

A casual pattern of various-sized stone pavers interspersed with mounds of flowering sedum creates a transition from the arid section of this garden to the more densely planted, lower-lying rain garden.

PATIOS, DECKS, AND TERRACES Hard surfaces may sound like the antithesis of gardening, but they have their virtues. We all need open areas in our gardens for outdoor living and to provide visual relief from planting beds, borders, and pots. Because hard surfaces are relatively weed free, long lasting, and unchanging through the seasons, they're low-maintenance.

Open-air dining and sitting rooms can be paved in gravel, pavers, concrete that lets water drain through, pebbles, crushed granite, or hazelnut shells. As a greater variety of recycled materials becomes available, we have more and more

An expansive cedar deck, topped with a sheltering arbor, captures outdoor living space on this steep property. Dry-stack stone walls retain the hillside and outline the deck.

interesting choices. Wooden decks are often used to extend the house out into the garden, but decking can also be used separate from the house as walkways or as destinations out in the garden.

PATHWAYS Pathways made of pavers, gravel, or other hard surfaces form the garden's navigational system. They also keep your feet dry and your shoes clean when you venture out in bad weather to check on your garden or pick some flowers. Be sure to make paths nice and wide—the rule of thumb is sufficiently wide for two people to walk side by side. At first this looks as bleakly bare as a German autobahn, but soon enough whatever you've planted as edging grows in to lap against the path, leaving just enough space to walk through the plants.

WATER FEATURES Ponds, pools, and streams also cover the ground, although they aren't particularly easy to maintain, requiring cleaning, repair, and often juggling to keep the balance of water and plants at a healthy ratio for clear water. However, water in the garden offers many pleasures. Fountains animate the garden with the sound of splashing and the bright glint of liquid. All water, moving or still, attracts birds, dragonflies, and other creatures, reflects the sky and passing

A bamboo fountain and squat stone basin add to this garden's quiet Asian aesthetics.

Most of the landscape designed by David Pfeiffer is built, paved, or studded with boulders, cutting maintenance to almost nothing through the seasons. In the entry, a rectangular pool is softened by stands of tall, narrow, native-looking reed grass.

clouds, warms up earlier than soil in springtime to get water plants off to a good start, and provides a spot to grow all kinds of fascinating plants that love wet roots. These satisfactions may offset the work involved, which may not seem so daunting when compared with maintaining the alternatives of lawns, ground covers, or even eco-lawns.

One way to enjoy water in the garden without all the work is to make your water feature the focus and keep the rest around it very simple and easy to take care of. Another strategy is to downsize the water feature—even birdbaths and dish rocks are reflective and attract creatures. A small recirculating fountain or a pot that drips water into a bed of stones at its base lends water music and motion to the garden, and you'll be surprised how quickly birds will flock to even the smallest water feature.

ECO-LAWNS Seed mixes have been developed to grow a ground cover that looks lawnlike without requiring as much mowing, edging, irrigating, or fertilizing as regular turfgrass. At their best, eco-lawns are casual, loose, and flowery and stay green all year, with various plants peaking, subsiding, and being replaced by fresh green. While they may never serve as a putting green or a croquet court, eco-lawns stand up well to dogs and kids, have a pleasant meadowy look, and stay green year-round (in most climates) without watering once they're established.

Be sure to use a seed mix formulated for your own region, developed with plants that dependably reseed and thrive in your climate. Ask your local extension agent for recommendations and check with larger nurseries to see if they carry region-appropriate seed mixes. Most mixes are a blend of annual and perennial grasses that aren't overly competitive, and low-growing, drought-resistant broadleaf plants.

The grasses are green and lush in winter and early spring when the herbaceous plants are weakest. The best types of grass to use depend on climate, but many mixes include perennial ryegrass and Kentucky bluegrass. The broadleaf plants—clovers (*Trifolium* species), common yarrow (*Achillea millefolium*), English daisies (*Bellis perennis*), and sweet alyssum (*Lobularia maritima*)—fill in during late summer drought when the grasses go dormant.

Add compost to the soil before planting. If your soil is heavy, you may need to add sand to the soil and/or install some drainage. Just like any other lawn, eco-lawns need sun to flourish.

RAISED BEDS Raised beds create instant topography in a garden, for they can be made in varying heights, sizes, and materials and arranged in patterns that delineate or divide up space. A series of raised beds separated by easy-care pathways (gravel, hazelnut shells, crushed granite) cover the ground to turn a garden with difficult soil or poor drainage into a productive, low-maintenance delight.

Raised beds can be as utilitarian as a low-lying grid of metal-framed boxes to improve soil and drainage, or they can be design features as in this rhythm of galvanized planters holding a screening of miscanthus and sedum. In both cases, the raised beds create topography and pattern, and they boost plant health and beauty.

GROUND COVERS A living mulch of plants—whether short little carpeting plants, drifts of perennials, or swaths of ornamental grasses—is one of the most eco-friendly and gorgeous ways to cover the ground. A garden of pathways wandering between slightly bermed beds of low-growing plants is textural, lush, wildlife friendly, and so gratifying to the gardener. Ground covers grow together to create cushiony green open areas that make up for the lawn they've replaced (we hope); many can even take foot traffic. Ground covers can be labor saving; when selected wisely for existing conditions and planted in well-prepared soil, ground covers take far less fertilizer and water than lawn grass, and don't need mowing, edging, or raking. Ground cover plantings are permeable, allowing water to percolate through the soil slowly rather than run off as storm water, which is especially problematic in our cities and suburbs.

Such sweeps of plants can also, however, be too labor intensive for a new low-maintenance garden. To cover the ground without creating a nightmare of work, keep weed control, plant care, and aggressiveness in mind.

Low-maintenance and drought-tolerant were the requirements for ground cover plantings in this seaside garden. Lavender, clumps of emerging *Sedum* 'Autumn Joy', and blue star creeper mounding up between the pavers couldn't be a simpler or more luscious trio of plants to carry this tough and hardy garden through the seasons.

Ground covers growing in the shade of an oakleaf hydrangea (*Hydrangea quercifolia*) lap at the edges of a hardscape of pavers and a millstone set into a circle of loose stones.

STRATEGIES FOR EASY-CARE GROUND COVERS

- Avoid plants that need deadheading, fertilizing, or dividing.
- Choose plants of similar timidity or vigor so that they'll coexist harmoniously, without one type or another dominating and crowding the others out. Overachievers may seem appealing at first because they spread quickly, but over time they cause too much trouble. It's worth tinkering to find compatible combinations, for nothing is lovelier than the overlapping textures and colors of ground covers that mingle compatibly.
- Plant ground covers more closely together than you might expect; for instance, small plugs of moss and thyme should be planted no more than your hand's width apart (which makes for easy measuring when planting). Avoid planting in even rows; staggered rows or a diamond pattern, or even random patterning, looks most natural as the plants grow in.
- Consider installing drip irrigation or soaker hoses to keep ground covers well watered, especially in the first few years, which will encourage them to cover the ground much more quickly.

- Mulch between freshly planted ground covers and pull weeds regularly until the plants are large enough and cover the ground enough to out-compete the weeds.

- When planting ground covers on a slope, choose strong, tough varieties that can withstand drought. Then carve out temporary little terraces, or angled trenches with a lip on the downhill side, to keep water from running off or eroding the soil away from the baby plants' roots. On a steep slope, you might need to reinforce these terraces with wooden bender board; on more gradual slopes this probably isn't needed.

- Any sharp, clean edge makes maintenance easier. Defining the edges of ground cover beds helps keep them tidy and the dirt from spilling over onto pathways, patios, or lawn. A clean edge of steel, aluminum, or wood edging strips, flagstones, or bricks slows down ground cover encroachment and helps keep plants and dirt where they belong.

- When planted in masses, ground covers can substitute for lawn, especially the "stepable" types like Irish moss, blue star creeper, and woolly thyme.

- Get the most visual impact from ground covers by combining them with hardscape. The textures and colors of the plants are shown off when lapping up against the edges of decks, patios, and terraces or growing around pavers. Planted in cracks and crevices, ground covers soften the edges of the hardscape as well as keep weeds out of difficult places.

- Ground covers and ground huggers aren't synonymous, so don't limit your thinking to low growers. Ferns, epimediums, hostas, ornamental grasses, lavender, and shorter bamboos work massed or interplanted to keep down weeds and cover the ground. Dwarf and prostrate conifers like the creeping English yew (*Taxus baccata* 'Repandens Aurea') and the tiny Norway spruce (*Picea abies* 'Little Gem') make easy-care, evergreen ground covers with great texture and personality.

For more plant suggestions, including a list of "stepables" and plants you should never, ever allow in your garden, see the "Smart Choices: Editing Your Plant Picks" chapter.

Black mondo grass grows slowly into large, effective clumps. The shiny, ebony foliage strikes a dark note in the garden, playing off all the shades of green.

FUSS-FREE TRANQUILITY: MARLENE SALON'S GARDEN OF GROUND COVERS

Have you ever noticed that fashion designers rarely wear the garments they sell but stick to a more pared-down, personal palette of clothes? Black jeans and turtlenecks, khakis and white shirts, or jeans and a T-shirt topped with a blazer are worn to make a statement day in and day out, with a minimum of thought and maintenance. These creatives find a formula that works for them, leaving the complications and expense of a designer wardrobe to . . . those who don't know better?

Oregon landscape architect Marlene Salon may design plant-rich gardens for her clients, but she's pursued simplicity in her fuss-free home garden. She relies

Landscape architect Marlene Salon's home garden is a low-maintenance green tapestry in every season, accented in summer with colorful heuchera and coleus growing in pots. A plant palette restricted to easy-care, shade-loving ground covers gives the garden a tranquil, Zen-like quality. The bluestone-paved main terrace functions as an outdoor sitting and dining room.

Sheets of textural groundcovers and mature shrubs fill the spaces between the rhythm of tree trunks and the repetition of water-filled basins in this simple yet sophisticated garden.

on swaths of ground cover to cut maintenance to nil. The result is an elegant, green-on-green tapestry perfectly suited to the conditions in her shady old garden, and to her family's time and interests. Her husband, David, is a lawyer. Says Marlene, "He calms himself by getting outside and gardening." A little pruning and snipping back of ground covers is a soothing flow of garden work, especially in such a quiet woodland garden rich in different leaf textures.

Marlene has even had the discipline to pare down the garden's décor to one repeated accent. She's placed huge circular basins, salvaged from old boiler parts, throughout the beds of ground covers, filling them to the brim with water from the hose. The basins' strong, simple shape and metal surfaces modernize the garden and light it up by reflecting sun and passing clouds. It's as if the basins draw the light and movement of the sky right down into the garden. Their watery surfaces ripple with every passing breeze, animating the garden. They also add a little height amidst the low-growing ground covers and create a strong visual rhythm, their repetition linking the various parts of the garden. There are six of these basins in the front garden, and each one is four feet across, so you can imagine the effect of all that reflective water undulating through the garden. The basins need only an occasional sweeping out with a broom and topping off with water from the hose to be kept looking their best.

Venerable old camellias, magnolias, witch hazels, a multistemmed katsura, and a stately, spreading Asian dogwood (*Cornus kousa*) form the garden's canopy. How many gardeners fight to garden in the rooty shade beneath such beautiful old shrubs and trees? Not Marlene. "I plant sheets of ground covers," she explains. "I use lots of epimedium, which grows and flowers just fine in the dry shade beneath all these established trees." Silky Japanese forest grass (*Hakonechloa macra*), which Marlene calls "a motherlode of a plant" for how easy it is to divide and spread about, has also thrived here. "We had patience but not a large budget, so we got lots of mileage out of one patch of these plants," says Marlene. She also covers the ground with masses of tough, sturdy plants like *Viburnum davidii*, evergreen ferns, and *Sarcococca ruscifolia*, which she loves for its sweet winter fragrance and shiny little leaves.

Despite the long-established feel of this third-of-an-acre city garden, Marlene and David have made many changes during their twenty-two years of residency. They began by removing nearly thirty trees. "And we still have a woodland garden!" says Marlene. They added a bluestone sitting area in the front garden, plus decks and an entry courtyard in simple geometric shapes to define the various spaces and make them more usable for eating and relaxing outdoors. "Most of what we've done is deletion," says Marlene. "Now we have a very restricted plant palette, for serenity and easy care."

Six shallow, water-filled metal basins, salvaged from old boiler parts, are nestled into the ground covers throughout the garden to reflect the sky and trees overhead.

Mulch Dos and Don'ts

Mulch, mulch, and more mulch is the commonest of garden mantras these days. It has been held up as the answer to all garden ills—mulch protects plants in winter, keeps down weeds, improves the soil, prevents water evaporation, and nurtures plants. While all this is true, the reality is that some mulches can damage plants, too.

Plant pathologist Olaf Ribeiro has found a worrisome variability in the mulches on the market. Some are devoid of micronutrients, while others carry active pathogens. He's found salt levels that he describes as "off the scales," adding, "Nothing will grow in this stuff." He's tested mulches by the truckload and by the bag, and found that even from the same company the quality varies wildly among different batches of mulch.

So what's a gardener to do? You can start by figuring out just what it is you're actually putting on your garden. Inexpensive pH kits have little strips that turn color (yes, it sounds like a home pregnancy test); if the mulch doesn't test between 5 and 7.5 it won't do much good. If you have a little more time, try tossing out quick-germinating bean or radish seeds. "If they keel over, there's a problem with the mulch," says Ribeiro with a laugh.

Mulches increase the soil's microbial activity, thus keeping plants healthy, but Ribeiro has found some mulches to be totally inert, meaning they contain nary a living organism. To make sure your brand of mulch is full of life, you can test it with a Solvita Soil Life Test (see "Resources" for ordering info). It's a simple kit for home gardeners that gives a reading on a mulch's vitality. And if you're buying a big batch of mulch from a garden center, be sure to ask them for a nutrient analysis. Reliable sources test their mulches.

HOW TO CHOOSE A MULCH Here's the simplest way to make sure your mulch is rich in the microbial activity that feeds plants and improves the soil: just choose mulch that contains aged manure. And to the burning question of what kind of manure is best for plants, Ribeiro replies that chicken manure is best, followed by cow, goat, and horse, in that order. Other experts, however, prefer steer or horse manure, suggesting that chicken manure is so high in phosphates that it inhibits beneficial microbes in the soil. What we do know for sure is that well-composted manure is beneficial to plants.

Since gardening is a visual medium for most of us, we can't help but consider how mulch looks as well as how it works. Mulch can look really messy, especially if it's full of twigs, or worse yet is a nasty orange color. Think about how mulch will look spread over beds and borders, particularly during the barer seasons of the year when it really shows up. Do you really want orange wood chips or raggedy-looking mulch covering much of your garden? Most organic matter has its virtues and drawbacks as mulch, but the hands-down best-looking mulch is bark mixed with aged manure. It looks like rich, dark, fluffy soil while it breaks down to make it so.

Mulches with high organic content, such as grass clippings and broken-down leaves and manure, are full of nutrients to feed your plants. The mulch decomposes over time, releasing these nutrients slowly in the soil, right where the plants' roots can easily soak them up. Worms do the work of breaking down the mulch, integrating it, to boost soil health and improve its consistency. Over time, you end up with soil that's fluffy and soft, with that delightful rich and fertile soil smell.

The dirty bottom line is to be cautious about what you put down in your garden. If all this sounds a bit daunting, be consoled that the big manufacturers, in an effort to be more consistent with their products, are sending batches of mulch to Ribeiro for testing and, we can hope, acting on his findings. But remember that mulching is worth all the effort, because when you top-dress your garden with mulch you're not only protecting your plants but also, through the mulch's microbial action, building a compost factory to improve the soil, long term, in a sustainable way.

HOW AND WHEN TO SPREAD MULCH First of all, weed thoroughly before mulching. If you don't, you'll be feeding the weeds! And if you're using a rich mulch, especially one with manure, keep it away from plants that prefer lean, dry soil, like lewisia, nasturtiums, lavender, rosemary, and other rock-garden and drought-tolerant plants that will smother in too much rich mulch.

The best time to apply a mulch, especially a "feeding" mulch (one that contains manure), is late winter before the bulbs are up so high their stems get in your way.

If you lay mulch down after a rain, you'll keep all that nice moisture in the soil. Depth matters—spread too thin, mulch fails to keep down weeds and disappears quickly. Spread too thick, it can smother plants and cause disease or rot when heaped up around the trunks and stems of woody plants. Two to four inches deep is ideal, with thinner application over crowns of perennials or clumps of ground cover. They like a little mulch, just not to be completely buried. And always keep mulch a few inches away from the base of trees and shrubs.

And I'm sorry to say, you can't spread it all with a rake. This works for most of the garden, but there will be places where you'll need to get down on your hands and knees and push mulch away from trunks (with thickly gloved hands, of course), move it about, and smooth it down. If this doesn't sound low-maintenance, remember you only need to do this once a year, and it's very satisfying work. In the weeks and months after mulching, make sure a crust doesn't form on the top of your mulch, for this will keep out the rain. If you notice the surface getting too hard, just scuffle it up a bit.

●

Mulching is probably the single best thing you can do to improve the looks and health of your garden. But it's important to choose mulch wisely and spread it correctly. The result will be healthier plants and soil, fewer weeds, and a tidy-looking garden.

ARTFUL SUSTAINABILITY: THE GARDENS OF CAMERON SCOTT

Seattle garden designer Cameron Scott is equal parts artist, innovator, and environmentalist. Cameron's a problem solver, retaining hillsides with recycled steel planters, crafting screens of recycled glass, and building minimum-footprint, maximum-productivity vegetable spirals out of recycled steel or copper. Creating garden features as beautiful and useful as they are sustainable ensures that his clients love their gardens and Cameron's designs over the long haul. Such durability goes beyond individual products and materials to be the most earth-friendly strategy of all.

Cameron points out that sustainability is a complicated and sometimes elusive concept. How much energy is used to produce something, and what by-products are created in its production? How far has a material been transported before it reaches your garden? He emphasizes a material's afterlife—how easy it is to deconstruct. Can it be used again in a different way? To this end, he uses

screws rather than nails so his constructions can be more easily and less destruc-
tively deconstructed.

Cameron's favorite sustainable techniques and materials include these:

- **Stone.** Local stone is his material of choice, for it's abundant, handsome, durable, and endlessly repurpose-able.

- **Water catchment.** "We live with rain many months of the year, so we may as well celebrate it," says Cameron of gardening and designing in the Northwest. He doesn't hide water in the landscape. By directing water into runnels, water-falls, ponds, and streams, he turns it into a living, moving, ever-changing feature of the landscapes he designs. Decorative rain chains harvest rain off the roof, directing it into rain barrels. Rainwater collected and stored in above-ground or underground cisterns can be used for irrigating the garden, flushing toilets, doing laundry. "It can take up to ten to twelve years to recover your investment in a total water catchment system, but if you bring the system inside to flush toilets, it's about eight years to payback," explains Cameron. He points out that the real payback lies in protecting municipal storm water sys-

The thirty-foot-long rain garden, which used to be a grassy slope, is now a feature of the Flotree garden. Rainwater runs down to percolate slowly through this natural depression planted with moisture-loving native plants.

Rain chains are beautiful and practical, celebrating the reality of rain while channeling it off the roof into a rain barrel or other catchment system.

tems from the overload that dumps pollutants into our lakes and streams, contaminating the water, killing fish, and ruining salmon spawning beds.

- **Concrete.** Cameron avoids using interlocking concrete blocks. "Besides looking hideous, they take so much energy to produce," he explains. He prefers concrete containing fly ash, a by-product of coal production, which makes the product more sustainable than typical concrete. It's an inexpensive replacement for the Portland cement usually used in concrete, and it actually increases the strength and ease of pumping concrete. Fly ash is also used in making concrete bricks, blocks, and pavers.

- **Raised beds.** Cameron says that more clients are requesting good-looking, creative ways to grow edibles. His solution of choice is raised beds. He's designed a clever, space-saving metal vegetable spiral and, depending on budget and aesthetics, also builds beds out of metal, stone, wood, and recycled steel.

Steel's advantages are its narrow, sleek profile; its cool, modern aesthetic; and its ability to help heat up the soil earlier in springtime. Weathering or architectural steel (commonly referred to by the U.S. Steel trade name Cor-Ten) takes on a rusty patina without ever rusting through. To prevent the

This hillside urban garden was badly in need of a facelift. Cameron brought it into the new millennium with powder-coated, recycled steel planters to retain the slope and update the old-fashioned rockery.

metal leaching into the soil, Cameron paints the inside of the beds with a natural rubber product.

Wood soaked in eco-friendly, nontoxic LifeTime Wood Treatment from Valhalla Wood Preservatives (see www.valhalco.com) is ideal for raised vegetable beds. Never use regular treated wood, as the coating leaches toxic chemicals into the soil.

Gabion walls are a strong and economical raised-bed solution. These wire-and-rock walls are an ancient concept that look coolly contemporary. Depending on what size stone you use to fill them, gabion walls can be built as narrow as four inches wide. Cameron suggests lining gabion-wall raised beds with landscape fabric to keep the soil from running out between the stones.

- **Construction.** Cameron uses renewable, exotic hardwoods like ipe to build decks, steps, walkways, and railings. The warm, rich color of ipe wood gives it a natural affinity with plants and the outdoors, and it holds up in any kind of weather. To cut down on maintenance, Cameron leaves the wood unfinished to weather naturally. How about the "manufactured wood" known as Trex? "It's garbage that ends up in landfills," says Cameron. "Ipe can be mulched in an afterlife."
- **Eco-lawns.** Cameron has found that the success of eco-lawns depends on soil

The shady garden has a green-on-green plant palette of easy-care Japanese forest grass, azaras, and oakleaf hydrangeas.

preparation; he amends soils for eco-lawns with 80 percent sand and 20 percent compost, but this depends on your mix and your conditions. It's worth experimenting with soil and mixes, because the loose, natural look of flowering eco-lawn is lovely. They need to be mowed infrequently and once established are irrigation-free.

Raised Bed Primer

Raised beds are an ancient concept, and they remain many a modern gardener's strategy of choice. These powerhouses of productivity are used in many areas of the world. Good soil and free drainage, conditions easier to achieve in raised beds, promote plant health and growth, as well as allowing plants to be grown more closely together. Raised beds are eco-friendly, for water and fertilizer use is minimized through the effectiveness of a more controlled root environment.

Planting beds raised above the level of the existing garden avoid the problem of bad soil or poor drainage, for you fill them with your own mix to suit the needs of the plants you want to grow. Raised beds are easier to tend because they're more comfortable to reach without bending over, an advantage at any age and a necessity for many gardeners. They're easier to design and easier to change out. Raised beds save on water and fertilizer because both can be directed just where they're needed. When I told a friend that my new garden was going to be mostly grown in raised beds, he asked me if I was planning ahead for when I got older, which made me laugh. I told him I wanted raised beds in my life right now!

And raised beds are more than merely practical. They can be arranged in pleasing patterns to become beautiful design features in and of themselves. In my garden, the raised beds run at an angle to visually widen the narrow back garden. They add height and topography to the garden and can be used to define and divide up garden spaces. Materials chosen, whether wood, metal, stone, or concrete, can set the style of the garden. Add a lip or shelf to the top surface of the bed for seating, whether for guests or for yourself while you garden.

Being raised up and corralled with a nice, hard edge not only makes plants look better, it keeps them healthier. Soil warms up earlier in springtime to get plants off to a good start. Slugs and snails have a harder time getting to the plants, and if you start with good, weed-free soil mix you'll have far fewer weeds, if any at all. Drainage is so much better, and soil can be custom tailored to plants' needs.

Plants that might well look a muddled mess combined in a larger bed somehow look great mingling together in raised beds. These beds are an ideal way to

Mixed-media artist Johanna Nitzke Marquis gardens in raised boxes not only to improve the soil and save her back but also to frame her garden's exuberance.

The vegetable spiral, or wedding cake raised bed, in Joan Caine's garden makes the most of every square inch of ground. The weathered steel is bulletproof, and the stacked-up soil warms up earlier in the season to give vegetables and herbs a springtime boost.

Raised beds as art—this poured concrete bed is colored a warm umber, crimped like a pie crust, and engraved with a favorite saying. "The garden is a transformer, poets know that," says artist-gardener Johanna Nitzke Marquis.

grow edibles, herbs, and flowers together, or to segregate edibles in the midst of an ornamental garden.

MATERIALS AND DIMENSIONS Choose among these materials, depending on cost and the look you want to achieve for your garden:

- **Stone.** Stone is both classic and classy. Line dry stacked stone with landscape fabric to prevent the soil from running out of the beds.
- **Concrete.** CMUs (concrete masonry units) mortared into place are strong, inexpensive, and fit most styles of garden. CMUs now comes in four-inch widths, so this economical material is now space-saving as well. Poured-in-place concrete is usually a more expensive route but can be customized in size, shape, and color.
- **Wood.** Never use treated wood, as it leaches toxic chemicals into the soil. Wood soaked in LifeTime Wood Treatment is long-lasting and nontoxic to plants.
- **Metal.** Recycled steel looks cool and contemporary while helping soil to heat up in spring. Where space is at a premium, steel has the narrowest profile, tak-

How often have you seen a structure so stunningly original yet dirt-gardening practical? Vegetables and herbs flourish in the curve of a bottomless raised bed crafted of recycled weathered steel.

ing up very little space. Feed troughs made of galvanized steel come in round or bullet shapes, which adds welcome curves or circle shapes to the mix. They heat up the soil quickly, have both an agrarian and modern aesthetic, and are inexpensive. Be sure to drill plenty of holes in the bottom so they don't rust. These can be found at feed stores.

- **Gabion walls.** These wire-and-stone walls are a strong and economical raised-bed solution. They work best when lined with landscape fabric, as with dry-stack stone walls.

Two feet high is a comfortable height for most gardeners, raising the soil up so you can easily reach into the bed to plant or pick. Two feet also gives adequate root depth to plant carrots and potatoes closely together, as well as for shrubs

and small trees. Raised beds can be any length that works for your garden, but keep the width under four feet, for wider than this makes the beds more difficult to work.

SOIL AND IRRIGATION Fill your raised beds with a compost-rich organic mix, which you can customize with the addition of various amendments

Galvanized steel feed troughs with plenty of holes drilled in the bottom make inexpensive raised beds large enough to grow a mix of pumpkins, flowers, and fruit.

depending on what plants you plan to grow where. Be prepared for shrinkage; for the first couple of years, you'll need to top off your beds every spring with more soil.

A simple, inexpensive drip system, or soaker hoses, will deliver the water to the roots of the plants, right where they need it.

Lawn Be Gone

Why are we so attached to our lawns? No other single garden element comes close to taking the time, attention, and resources that turfgrass demands. You'd think all that mowing, fertilizing, weeding, watering, and edging would end our love affair with lawns. Even if we let it go brown in the summers, lawn still uses far more water than we should be pouring into the soil, let alone the chemical fertilizer and herbicide run-off that poisons our waterways and fish.

I cringe when I see lawns growing in desert climates or covering vast suburban landscapes. Can you imagine a more frightening sight than those little flags, stuck in lawns and parking strips, warning that this lawn has just been sprayed with dangerous chemicals? I remember when whole neighborhoods were littered with such scary little flags. Why would anyone want children or pets to play on surfaces drenched in poison?

Lawn is a monoculture, and a greedy one at that. Cutting down on or ridding your property of lawn is the single most effective way to reduce your gardening footprint in terms of your own work, impact on those around you, and use of the earth's resources.

Thank goodness, ridding properties of lawn is a growing trend. Whether it's because we're looking for more privacy in our increasingly crowded neighborhoods or because we're digging up lawn to plant vegetables, gardeners are ridding themselves of the yoke of caring for turfgrass. They're finding fresh ways to cover the ground. But first we need to get rid of the grass.

You can slowly whittle away your lawn, digging wider beds and borders until the turf disappears altogether. Or you might prefer to get rid of big swaths of lawn all at once. No matter how you approach cutting down on lawn, you can save your back and improve your soil at the same time with the "no dig" method of garden transformation.

Autumn is the perfect time to begin the process, and by spring when plant lust is upon you, beds full of fluffy soil will be ready and waiting. A supply of newspapers or cardboard, a shovel, mulch, and four to six months is all that's needed to transform turfgrass into ready-to-plant soil. The joy and genius of this simple method is that time and nature do most of the work.

KILLING YOUR LAWN IN FIVE EASY STEPS

1. Begin by digging a shallow ditch about four inches wide and four inches deep outlining the edges of the future border. Throw the dirt and grass dug from this moat onto the lawn you plan to get rid of—it becomes part of the mulch.

2. Cover all the grass you want to eliminate with a single layer of cardboard (broken-down boxes are fine) or a half-inch-thick layer of newspapers (or newsprint—which is newspaper without the ink—if you're squeamish about inks in the garden), overlapping each layer by four to six inches and letting the edges fall down into the little ditch. Now the grass is completely covered with a solid layer of cardboard or newspapers. You can water them to keep them in place until you get to step 3.

3. Now it's time for the mulch, which should be leaves, grass clippings, compost, purchased mulch, or a combination of all four. Cover the paper layer with an eight-to-twelve-inch-deep layer of the mulch. Now you have a mound of mulch, trimmed with a trench, that you can ignore until spring.

4. Let it all rot down for four to six months. No air or light will penetrate to the grass, so it will die, roots and all. The mass will shrink by more than half on its way to becoming great planting soil.

5. In the spring, top off the new planting areas with several fresh inches of a feeding mulch (a mixture of bark and manure available in bulk or bags from a nursery or garden center) and you're ready to plant into the rich soil of your new beds and borders.

Chris Bedner and Dan Ostrowski, framed in Japanese anemones, are enjoying their revamped garden, which offers privacy, outdoor living spaces, and year-round beauty with a minimum of maintenance.

OPPOSITE: A lush carpet of hostas, hellebores, ferns, and acanthus thrive in the shade of redbuds and oaks in this Arlington Virginia, garden, transformed by designer Tom Mannion from sunny lawn to private, easy-care oasis.

FROM OPEN LAWN TO LOW-MAINTENANCE PRIVACY: THE BEDNER-OSTROWSKI NO-MOW GARDEN

"I'm a putterer," says Chris Bedner of her love for getting outdoors and working in the garden. But after she and her new husband, Dan Ostrowski, remodeled their Arlington, Virginia, home, Chris longed for a new style of garden. "I grew up on four acres in the country, and I didn't want to mow anymore," she says.

The couple's small lot was typically suburban with its wide-open lawn, hedges of camellias, and shrubby azalea foundation plantings. Chris wanted more privacy, an outdoor dining room, and a plant-rich garden. She hoped for a garden that took care of itself when need be yet afforded space for her to get out there and plant her favorite fragrant lilies and daphnes. And she longed for an outdoor space so gracious and inviting it'd coax family and visitors out into the garden. Yet she also longed to ditch the lawnmower and didn't want to spend as much time and effort on gardening as she had in the past.

Landscape designer Tom Mannion to the rescue. Chris's program for her garden came as no surprise. "Clients *always* ask for low-maintenance—it's just part of the territory," Mannion explains. How to create a lush and beautiful garden that is easy to care for? Mannion rattles off a list: Reduce or eliminate lawn. Eliminate plants that need staking or spraying. No hedges that need tight trimming to look good. Repeat plantings. And he relies on the structure of the hardscaping, rather than evergreen plants, for winter interest. This strategy leaves more room for the seasonal theatrics of favorite deciduous plants, like hydrangeas and Japanese snowbell trees (*Styrax japonica*).

Mannion believes that the gardener shouldn't have to referee between competing plants. "That's just too much work," he says. When a garden is well designed, the homeowner's tasks should be the pleasurable ones of witnessing and editing the ebb and flow of plants through the seasons. Which is just what Chris loves to do, what she describes as her "puttering."

"Now we have lovely stone paths and a patio in back just large enough for our dining table and chairs," says Chris. The burgundy heart-shaped leaves of 'Forest Pansy' eastern redbud (*Cercis canadensis*), oaks, and venerable old camellia hedges create leafy privacy in this now pleasantly shady garden.

Bluestone paving and a surround of shrubs and trees creates a private outdoor room. Effective, easy-care focal points of Japanese forest grass (*Hakonechloa macra* 'Aureola') in simple terra cotta pots light up the shady garden with their golden glow.

Mannion's plant palette is so textural you'd never notice it's repetitive, making the garden a breeze to care for. "I love all the varieties of green. It's a great mix of hellebores, hostas, ferns, and Solomon's seal," says Chris. Favorite plants like autumn fern (*Dryopteris erythrosora*), sweet spire (*Itea virginica*), serviceberry, liriope, hardy geraniums, and nandina are repeated throughout the garden, creating a harmonious picture as well as ease of maintenance.

"We didn't sacrifice anything for low-maintenance," says Chris. "This is the most carefree garden, but when I step outdoors it feels like I'm in a park." Chris appreciates that Tom Mannion chose plants that thrive in the garden's existing conditions. "We wanted natural, local plants that would grow well here," she says. Mannion lightened up the garden with white-flowering plants like *Styrax japonica* and 'Annabelle' hydrangeas. "He gave me a white garden," exclaims Chris as if surprised by her garden's beauty five years after planting. "Had I known I wanted one, I would have asked for it."

Mannion's design and plantings passed a very tough test. "I was diagnosed with cancer," says Chris. "I'm okay now, but for those two years the garden just grew and took care of itself."

Casual seating areas feel almost Zenlike in the quiet simplicity of their curved benches and green plant palette.

Weeds Are History

Weeds are the number-one complaint of gardeners, which is no surprise, for the pesky buggers impact both the looks and health of our gardens. Weeds are a formidable foe, for they seem to possess the pent-up life force of the universe in their vigorous stems and seeds. They'll outlive us all with their daunting vigor. Some, like horsetails, have been around since the days of the dinosaurs. But wouldn't it be nice if we could just subdue them enough so we could enjoy our gardens in the meantime? Who wants to spend time weeding when you could be planting, harvesting, or relaxing in the garden?

It's possible, with know-how and persistence (and without using toxic chemicals), to tame weeds to the point where it's a satisfying pleasure to go out and pull a few because it's such a rare task. Honest. You won't find any information on chemicals in this book, as they are unquestionably bad for the soil, water, creatures, and our own health (see "Keep It Green" in the next chapter).

Here are some strategies to fight the good fight and win the war against weeds:

- **Start right.** The number-one tip from the gardeners I spoke with is to buy a weed-free property to begin with. When you're house shopping, check out the garden carefully for any sign of horsetails, bindweed, or other pesky perennial weeds. Then keep these plagues at bay by thoroughly vetting any soil, compost, or mulch you import, as well as the soil around the roots of plants you acquire, particularly ones given to you from other people's gardens. These are the usual ways weeds infiltrate gardens, and it's much easier to keep them out in the first place.

- **Enrich the soil.** Improving your soil boosts the health of the plants you're cultivating while eliminating conditions encouraging to weeds. Solve drainage problems with French drains, ditches, or drainpipe to eliminate the many weeds, like horsetail, that do best in damp conditions. Adding organic matter, compost, and aged manure improves soil tilth and boosts its fertility, which is good for the plants you want and discourages the ones you don't want.

- **Apply mulch.** A three-to-four-inch-thick layer of mulch, applied between and around plants spring and fall, breaks down to improve the soil, smothering weeds in the meantime. Don't heap mulch over the crowns of perennials, and

OPPOSITE: Pachysandra and hostas are repeated throughout the garden for their ease of maintenance and shade-loving ways.

"I love a garden that is impossibly lush, that requires editing but not refereeing. The gardener is there to witness and edit the ebb and flow but not to referee. That's too much work."

–Tom Mannion, garden desiger

keep it a couple of inches away from the trunks and stems of trees and shrubs.

- **Cover the ground.** Leave no bit of soil bare, for weeds are opportunists just waiting to move right in. Plant carpeting ground covers or lay down gravel, stones, pavers, or black Japanese stone to cover the ground.
- **Pull weeds early.** Weed easy, weed early (like shifting a bike before going up a hill). Pull weeds before they mature and disperse their seeds, because we don't even like to think about the gazillions of babies each weed can produce if left alone to bloom and reproduce. Don't let it happen.
- **Persist in pulling the suckers.** Like any other plant, weeds need light and air to thrive. If you pull them and pull them again, they'll decline in vigor. Persist and don't be discouraged. Weeding has its benefits, for it gets you down there at eye level to keep track of what's going on with your plants—and it's enormously satisfying to clean out a planting bed in springtime or rid a gravel drive or terrace of weeds.
- **Fry them.** Earth-friendly, nonchemical aids to weed control include spraying with vinegar, pouring boiling water on weeds, or, my personal favorite, incinerating the interlopers with a blast from a flame torch.
- **Dispose of weeds in the garbage.** Don't count on your home compost to heat up enough to destroy weed seeds and roots. In fact, spreading composted weeds about the garden is a sure way to cause even more of a problem. Keep weeds out of the compost. It's best to bag them, tie the bag securely, and put it in the garbage.
- **Smother the whole lot.** Sometimes it's easier to smother the whole lot of them than pull weeds out one by one. In my current garden, the drainage is so bad and the horsetails so pervasive that we covered most of the ground with thick black landscape cloth, generously overlapped at the seams and held down with a thick gravel mulch. I garden in lovely weed-free soil in pots and raised beds on top of the gravel. Weed seeds blow in and some of my plants seed about, but the perennial weed scourge has been defeated.

Keep It Simple

- Learn to tolerate imperfection—remember that gardens are outdoors, part of nature, and never meant to be perfect. If you don't obsess over pulling every weed and raking every leaf, your garden will be healthier and you will be too.

- Soil is key to a low-maintenance garden. Enriching and improving your garden's soil does double duty. It boosts the health of the plants you're cultivating while discouraging weeds by altering the soil conditions they prefer. Learn what kind of soil you're working with by getting a low-cost soil test. The best $9 you can spend is to send a sample of your garden soil to the University of Massachusetts at Amherst for analysis. (Details in "Resources.")

- Compost adds fertility and life to soil, as it improves drainage and soil structure. Compost feeds earthworms, buffers toxins in the soil, and helps plants to resist diseases and insect pests. And to think this powerhouse of a soil amendment is created naturally as yard waste and kitchen scraps break down—a natural process that goes on all the time with little or no help from us.

- If you don't have the time or inclination for lab tests, go with the mulch that is most dependable and improves both the looks and function of your garden. Bark mixed with well-aged manure, whether you buy it in bulk or bags, looks like dark, rich soil. Chicken manure is best for plants; second best is steer. Spread thickly (three to four inches deep), it keeps down weeds, insulates plants from cold winter weather, and in summer helps keep soil from drying out. Even better, it breaks down to feed plants and improve the soil.

- As with anything else in life, attitude matters. Don't manage your garden for problems, but for your successes, and build on them. Gardeners who continually fret over pests and diseases, rather than pulling out malingering plants and getting rid of them, don't enjoy their gardens very much. Pay close attention to which plants take naturally to the conditions in your garden and plant more of them. Succeed, repeat, succeed again.

- Put most of your energies into the areas of your garden you see close up and most often, such as front and back doors, walkways, patios, decks, and containers. Keep these spruced up and weed free, and your garden will give an overall well-groomed impression.

- If you garden a large piece of property, think in terms of maintenance zones. Perhaps a patio area, deck, or front walkway is used enough to justify containers, fussier plants, more work. Further out zones can be dedicated to eco-lawn, sweeps of ground cover, or swaths of native plants that take far less care and fewer resources. A California garden designed by Vanessa Kuemmerle has a simple hardscaped living and dining room sheltered by eight-foot-tall stucco walls. Outside of the walls, the slope is thickly planted in drought-tolerant South African plants that take little care. In Cheryl Kamera's intensely planted island garden, she carved a tranquil little terrace out behind her gardening shed where she could sit and relax and enjoy the garden and not feel beset by chores.

Resources

Gardening is local, which means homegrown resources are your best bet. Nearly every county in the United States has a master gardener program offering up-to-date information through free clinics and free or low-cost publications. Ask at neighborhood nurseries and public libraries to find out where master gardener clinics are held in your area, or google "Master Gardeners, ___ County." Ask other gardeners where they find reliable gardening information. Check out weekly gardening calendars in your newspaper. One of the very best and most enjoyable ways to learn about gardening is to join local gardening groups, for they offer not only camaraderie with like-minded people but also newsletters and lectures for their members.

In addition to books published regionally, the books and online resources listed here are filled with practical, down-to-earth advice for beginning and seasoned gardeners alike.

BOOKS   *Down to Earth with Helen Dillon: Advice and Inspiration from One of the World's Great Gardeners* by Helen Dillon (Timber Press, 2007). Irish dirt gardener Dillon gets down in this book filled with wisdom on everything from the best plants to dealing with dogs in the garden. At its best, the book is like having a conversation with your best gardening friend, who just happens to have a great sense of humor and a vast love and knowledge of everything garden.

The Garden Primer: The Completely Revised Gardener's Bible by Barbara Damrosch (Workman, 2008). No matter your gardening question, whether it's when to plant Belgian endive or how to force paperwhites, this impressively fat and

A quiet patio centered with a bubbling fountain gives respite to both visitors and the gardener herself on an intensely planted multiacre property.

Behind the walls, the garden
is lush with plants; the outdoor
living room is simplicity itself.

thorough book is the place to start. The appendix is stuffed with sources of plants and seeds, a climate zone map, and a list of plant societies. It leans toward edibles, is 100 percent organic, and has a detailed index and clear illustrations.

The Illustrated Encyclopedia of Trees by David More (Timber Press, 2002). Worth the price just for the illustrations, let alone the wealth of information. You'll find colored drawings of tree shapes and profiles, twigs, leaves, fruit, nuts, berries, and flowers. This tome on trees is catnip to anyone who loves detailed botanical drawings.

The Informed Gardener by Linda Chalker-Scott (University of Washington Press, 2008). A professor of urban horticulture takes on gardening myths by offering clear, concise, and up-to-date information and research. No, she doesn't believe in the efficacy of compost tea; yes, you should rough up root balls when you transplant . . . and much more.

Tending Your Garden: A Year-Round Guide to Garden Maintenance by Gordon and Mary Hayward (Norton, 2007). The personal tone and husband-and-wife teamwork that's gone into the couple's Vermont garden for more than twenty-five years makes the topic of maintenance more interesting than you'd expect. If you're daunted by the Haywards' thirty-hour work week (each) as well as the twenty-five hours put in by their helpers (only hired since the couple turned sixty), you'll understand the reason I wrote this book.

Time-Saving Gardener: Tips and Essential Tasks, Season by Season by Carolyn Hutchinson (Firefly Books, 2008). This might well be the book you carry around the garden with you. It offers in clear prose, photos, and plenty of detailed drawings the kind of gardening information we wish we'd learned at our parents' or grandparents' knees. If planting carrots, making compost, and recognizing vine weevils aren't second nature, this book's for you. It's arranged seasonally and takes an organic approach to problem solving.

A Year on the Garden Path: A 52-Week Organic Gardening Guide, Second Edition by Carolyn Herriot (EarthFuture Publications, Victoria BC, Canada, 2005). This is a family and earth-friendly seasonal guide to soulful, heartfelt gardening, filled with lists, tips, and tricks worth referring to again and again.

ONLINE RESOURCES **Frugal Gardening**, www.frugalgardening.com, could have spent a little more money on Web page design, but it's saved from its stodgy look by offering all those tips and tricks we wish our parents or grandparents had taught us. If you're flexible, assertive, creative, and patient, you're the perfect frugal gardener, according to the site. The topics are amazingly varied, from using vinegar in the garden to harvesting rainwater and repurposing objects for garden use. The main writer lives and gardens in the Northwest.

Garden Rant, www.gardenrant.com, is just that—a quartet of voices from dedicated gardeners bored with perfect magazine gardens and determined not to take it anymore. Amy Stewart, author of *Flower Confidential* (Algonquin Books, 2007), is the best known of the group, but all are feisty, opinionated, full of good humor and passion for plants and gardens. And did I mention opinionated? This is one of the most visited gardening blogs out there, for it's like talking to a bunch of keen gardening friends who just happen to be professional bloggers. Do yourself a favor and check out the section called "Designs, Tricks, and Schemes."

Pervious Concrete's Web site, www.perviouspavement.org, makes the case for how vital it is for water to percolate down through the natural filter of our garden soil. You'll be out busting up pavement, inspired by all the good-looking ideas for alternative permeable surfaces.

University of Massachusetts, Amherst, Soil and Plant Tissue Testing Laboratory, www.umass.edu/plsoils/soiltest/, offers a standard soil test that identifies your soil's pH, available nutrients, and any heavy metals present. Highly recommended as the best and least expensive soil test available. The thorough Web site supplies all the information you need to send in a soil sample.

A Way To Garden, www.awaytogarden.com, is blogging at its best, with glorious photos and the strong, personal voice of Margaret Roach, who for fifteen years served as garden editor and then executive editor for *Martha Stewart Living* magazine. Roach left corporate life to stay at home in rural New York, where she gardens and blogs, gardens and blogs, and we're all the richer for it. Her work is a model of brevity, seasonality, and love of plants and nature, all written in a voice so full of joy in her new life that it makes eschewing words written on paper worthwhile, for a few minutes anyway.

Woods End Laboratories in Mount Vernon, Maine, www.woodsend.org, sells the Solvita Soil Life Test I recommend using to make sure the mulch you apply to your garden is full of life. This simple kit gives a reading on a mulch's vitality.

www.mastercomposter.com. Gives simple instructions on how to compost yard and kitchen waste. See also *The Green Gardener's Guide*, listed in the "Resources" section in the next chapter.

This small urban Bedner-Ostrowski garden is so rich in textural plantings and so private, you'd never know neighbors were close at hand. Every bit of ground is covered with paving or plants to reduce maintenance to sweeping and a little early spring cleanup.

Nature's Rhythms

WHETHER YOU CALL IT SUSTAINABLE, green, or organic, gardening in tune with nature is the ultimate in low-maintenance smarts. Fighting against the realities of your climate and soil is a losing battle, as well as an expensive one in terms of time, money, and environmental damage. Think of all the water, fertilizers, pesticides, and herbicides that over the years have gone into making grass grow in desert climates and boosting shrubs and trees that are not adapted to where they've been planted.

This synthetic approach to gardening is wastefully unsustainable. It turns gardeners into plant slaves and plants into fertilizer junkies. If your garden is ever going to be more independent, it needs to get back in tune with Mother Nature.

Nature herself gives plenty of clues on how to be a successful gardener with minimal effort. Watch where the sun falls across your property, where the frost lingers or the soil stays damp most of the time. Through patient observation you learn which plants will grow happily and easily in which location, where to mound soil up in berms or build raised beds for decent drainage, or where to take advantage of a boggy spot by digging a pond or planting moisture-loving plants that will thrive in soggy soil.

ABOVE: Shirley poppies

OPPOSITE: Garden owner and designer Jennifer Carlson broke up an old concrete slab, replacing it with a permeable patio of aggregate pavers bisected by ribbons of beach stones. The patterning of the new patio is more textural and inviting, while reducing runoff by allowing water to percolate through.

"I think being modern is being aware of the political aspects of both horticulture and agriculture—and refusing to buy pesticides, chemical fertilizers, and genetically modified seeds that do not 'feed the world,' as we have been told, but pollute the land, kill soil organisms, and support the oil industry. Gardeners can do a lot to reclaim the earth, politically and biologically."

–Anne Raver, New York Times garden columnist

Garden writer and philosophy professor Allen Lacy famously said, "Garden where you live," which isn't as obvious as it sounds. How many gardens have you seen that appear to deny the reality of geography and weather? Not that you can't indulge in a little zonal denial, but you pay for such fantasies in labor and cost.

Gardening where we live doesn't mean we must grow only native plants. I think what Lacy means is that gardeners must first understand and accept the realities of their cold, hot, humid, soggy, or droughty gardening conditions. This is the starting place for all environmentally responsible, lower-maintenance gardening. No point in growing eggplants, no matter how you love their taste, if the summers where you live never get much above 80 degrees F—eggplants and a host of other fruits and vegetables need reliable heat to ripen. What's the last frost date in your area, how long is the typical growing season, when does the first frost hit? All this information is available online and from your local extension agent, who should become your new best friend.

Our gardens ground us in our natural environment and give us a sense of place—but only if we understand and acknowledge what that place really offers us as gardeners.

Keep It Green

Chemical fertilizers and pesticides have no place in our gardens. Homeowners have actually dumped more pollutants into the environment with their heedless gardening practices than have farmers and agribusiness. These professionals watch amounts and dollars more carefully than those of us at home, who tend to spray here and there, or worse yet, hire "need-it-or-not" routine spraying services. My fervent wish is to never again see those little white warning flags on freshly-doused-with-poison gardens. And I won't go back into any of the big box stores until they're free of that horrid chemical smell emanating from the gardening aisles.

Have you ever thought how counter-intuitive it is for gardening aisles to stink like poison? How noxious all those kill-the-bugs and fry-the-weeds substances must be to stink up a store like that! How can gardeners consider carrying such substances home and applying them to the garden, where our children, dogs, and cats play, and where butterflies, hummingbirds, and robins flit about, nest, sip nectar, and poke about looking for worms?

The tobacco industry assured us of the safety of cigarettes back in the 1950s, just as the chemical industry assures us today that their poisons are harmless. Ever since Rachel Carson exposed chemical industry lies in 1962 in *Silent Spring*, we've known the horrendous effects chemicals have on our environment. Why are we still buying and using this stuff? Why are we permitting our municipalities to spray roadsides and douse public landscapes?

When I took master gardener training twenty years ago, many of the classes were about how to use herbicides and pesticides most effectively. When I joined the Garden Writers Association fifteen years ago, I promptly quit because my mailbox was stuffed with advertising from Ortho. Neither of these things is true anymore, which gives me great hope for a healthy gardening future.

Chemical fertilizers and pesticides have been linked to contamination of drinking water and to serious health risks to children, adults, and animals. But here's the crazy thing—poisons really have nothing to do with making gardens. They're not necessary for growing healthy, beautiful gardens. In fact, poisons are a detriment because they sterilize the soil and kill off the good bugs just as surely as the bad. Isn't it just common sense to feed the soil with compost and the healthy living biota found in manure, and then let the plants feed on that banquet of micronutrients?

Healthy plants resist disease and insect infestation. The best way to keep your plants healthy is to locate them where they get the kind of sun, water, and soil that suits them best, then leave them alone to grow and thrive. If they falter and decline, attracting insects and disease, pull them out and start over. There are plenty of other good plants to try that will do better in the conditions offered by your garden.

And just in case you have any lingering desire to reach for a chemical solution when faced with garden challenges, consider these frightening facts from the nonprofit organization Environment and Human Health, Inc. (www.ehhi.org):

- Commonly used lawn-care chemicals can persist in soil, the air we breathe, and water for weeks, which can lead to the contamination of aquatic resources and local wildlife.
- Increased odds of childhood leukemia, brain cancer, and soft tissue sarcoma have been associated with children living in households where pesticides are used.
- Some inert ingredients in pesticides are suspected carcinogens; others have

"To me the key thing about modern gardens is the way they work together with nature but not in a narrow way that's just about looking 'natural.' They can be formal, stylized, but the design is underpinned by ecological principles that tie the garden into the locality and seasons."

–Joanna Fortnam, deputy gardening editor, Telegraph Media Group, London

been linked to central nervous system disorders, liver and kidney damage, birth defects, and some short-term health effects.

● The use of pesticides often harms wildlife and their habitats, as well as pets. Both dogs and cats are known to eat grass. There have been many cases of pets' deaths from lawn treatments.

● In addition to contaminating surface water, pesticides can contaminate groundwater, potentially causing health problems for people drinking it.

PRETTY IS AS PRETTY DOES: JENNIFER CARLSON'S SUSTAINABLE GARDEN

Sustainable gardens can be as beautiful as they are virtuous. There's nothing even remotely granola or Birkenstock about Jennifer Carlson's little urban Seattle garden. Her strategies, philosophies, and techniques apply to any style of garden and to any climate, be it high desert, woodland, or coastal. You'd never guess to look at it that this earth-friendly haven, with all its animals and edibles, is more akin to a working farm than a typical city garden. But its small-scale, well-thought-out structures and carefully placed plants make it as easy to care for as it is productive.

Trained as an artist and landscape architect, Jennifer runs a design-build firm, teaches classes, and consults on sustainable gardens. No wonder she's designed her garden to nearly take care of itself. "I'm out here just five times a year to deadhead, weed, and clip back," explains Carlson of her tough-love regime. "The rest of the time the plants need to shine on their own." She repeats tough, durable plants throughout the garden, adding in plenty of edibles and herbs, as well as native plants to feed and shelter birds and other wildlife.

Jennifer's goal is to recycle all waste generated by her plants and animals right here in her own garden, and to capture and reuse rainwater for all the garden's irrigation needs. While Jennifer's sustainable loop philosophy may be cutting-edge green, it's grounded in the history and realities of place. When Jennifer and her family moved to their new home six years ago, she set about carefully researching her property's physical history. She began with the big picture, studying where the sun falls, the composition of the soil, how water flows and where it collects. From topography to maintenance, Carlson pondered how each part of

By summer, Jennifer's narrow side garden grows into an edible tunnel, with four kinds of rhubarb, figs, and artichokes, garnished with poppies, daphne, and spirea for flowers and color through the seasons.

the garden could be built, engineered, or planted so that it adds up to one integrated, sustainable whole. From composting fence to permeable patio and chicken tractor, every eco-savvy element in the Carlson garden contributes to her garden's sustainability.

Here are Jennifer's sustainable strategies:

- **Build healthy soil.** Jennifer's first task in crafting a sustainable garden lay beneath her feet. As soon as she'd ripped out ivy, overgrown shrubs, and a dead cherry tree, she set about building healthy soil. "Every week I'd take in a couple of empty buckets to the neighborhood coffee café and exchange them for two full buckets of coffee grounds," says Carlson. She removed lawn to widen the beds, dug in compost and coffee grounds, and started planting. Because her plants got off to such a good start and are frequently mulched, they require very little care to look their best.

- **Make hard surfaces permeable.** As with many older houses, the patio was a solid slab of concrete, which wasn't particularly attractive and didn't allow water to percolate through the soil slowly. Jennifer broke it up and replaced it with pavers separated by ribbons of stones to allow water to drain.

- **Use sunshine productively.** Raised beds are tucked in the garden's sunniest spot between garage and fence; the garage is painted a dark color to maximize reflected heat, which helps to ripen peppers and eggplant.

- **Catch rainwater.** Carlson collects enough water (four thousand gallons) from half her thousand-square-foot roof to water her entire garden, including lawn

Between September and May, Carlson harvests more than 4000 gallons of rainwater off the roof of the house, storing it in three 625-gallon cisterns to water the garden over the summer.

and vegetables. She attaches a hose or hooks up a sprinkler to the three dark green polypropylene cisterns, 625 gallons each, lined up against the back fence. "I've never used it all up over the summer" says Jennifer proudly of her free source of irrigation water.

- **Keep chickens.** The three Buff Orpington hens are moved around the garden in a bottomless "chicken tractor" pen, which protects and contains them while they turn over the soil and fertilize the lawn. The tractor is built of recycled cedar and hardware cloth; at night, the chickens return to the safety of their permanent hen house.

Three Buff Orpington hens contribute eggs for eating as well as manure and bedding to improve the soil. Carlson moves them around the garden in their own "tractor," a floorless portable hybrid between cage and cart, distributing their tasks of turning up the soil and fertilizing throughout the garden. At night, the hens are returned to the safety of their colorful home coop.

- **Plant appropriately.** Every shrub, tree, and perennial is vetted for drought tolerance and durability. "My criteria are interesting color, leaf shape, and texture," says Jennifer. "My plants require minimal pruning, and many offer wildlife habitat." A short list of Jennifer's favorite plants include vine maple (*Acer circinatum*), flowering currant (*Ribes sanguineum*), and Pacific wax myrtle (*Myrica californica*). She favors small shrubs like *Viburnum davidii*, *Spirea*

A narrow garden bed holds three kinds of fruit. Recently planted pear, apple, and Italian prune plum trees are espaliered along a slim fifteen-foot-long fence. Beneath them, Carlson has layered blueberries with a ground cover of strawberries to shade their roots.

When layer upon layer of yard waste is stuffed into the composting fence, it looks almost like a stratified archeological or geological find. But this clever fence is thoroughly modern. Jennifer designed and built it with the help of her husband and son, out of cedar posts and cattle wire, and topped it with an arbor draped in kiwi and grapes.

japonica 'Magic Carpet', and yellow boxleaf honeysuckle (*Lonicera nitida* 'Baggesen's Gold'), mingling with the long-blooming geranium 'Rozanne', the hardy autumn fern (*Dryopteris erythrosora*), variegated Japanese sedge (*Carex oshimensis* 'Evergold'), and plenty of easy-care euphorbia and sedum.

- **Layer edibles.** A fifteen-foot-long espaliered fruit tree fence yields pears, apples, and Italian prune plums. Every inch of land is productive; blueberries are layered beneath the little fruit trees, with a ground cover of strawberries shading the blueberry roots.

- **Create a composting fence.** Carlson stretched parallel rows of cattle wire between cedar posts to create a contained space about a foot wide for stuffing in layers of yard clippings and debris. It's the ultimate in double-duty structures—in fact, it serves quadruple duty. When filled with debris, it functions as a privacy screen, its layers looking interestingly archaeological. Most pruning debris fits neatly into the fence, so it doesn't need to be hauled off the property. Wrens and chickadees are attracted to the decomposing vegetation, which over time breaks down and sloughs out the bottom of the fence to feed all the plants growing close by.

- **Incorporate repurposed materials.** Jennifer built the chicken coop, rabbit hutch, and aviary out of recycled pallets and lumber. Most of the garden structures, like fences and arbors, are built of recycled cedar. Perhaps the ultimate in recycling are all the rocks Carlson has carried home after sifting them out of the soil in her clients' gardens to use as part of her patio design to increase permeability.

- **Accept critters' contributions.** Even the creatures that live in this busy garden are multitaskers. Take the fluffy angora rabbit brothers, Peaches and Mocha. Their alfalfa hay bedding and droppings are composted to fertilize the garden, and Carlson gathers and spins their fur. Other colorful coops and hutches hold the three hens, cooing doves, and a quail, all of which contribute eggs to eat and manure and bedding to improve the soil.

The rabbit hutch in Jennifer Carlson's garden sports a green roof and is built of recycled lumber. Angora rabbit brothers Peaches and Mocha are an integral part of the garden's circle of sustainability, for their manure is used as fertilizer and their alfalfa hay as mulch. Jennifer harvests their hair for spinning.

Flora Non Grata; or, Don't Unleash the Beasts

For every gardener who deplores Japanese anemones, bronze fennel, or *Ranunculus ficaria* 'Brazen Hussy' as too aggressive, there are ten more who love plants that spread about so willingly. Every area of the country has its own kudzu, a menace of a plant that's escaped to choke out native plants and invade wildlands, creating a bleak and unhealthy monoculture.

Noxious weeds are defined as nonnative plants that are aggressive, competitive, and highly destructive. They usually lack natural enemies and resist methods of control. Many have escaped from gardens to destroy natural plant and animal habitat with their suffocating ways. Each state has its own noxious weed list, easily located online.

But beyond plants that are on that list, there are many more that are potential problems. So how to be responsible gardeners without giving up nature's self-seeding bounty and the excitement of trying out new plants?

I think the defining question is this: Which plants are management issues within our garden, seeding about too freely, or spreading more vigorously than we'd prefer, and which are a danger to our parks and woodlands? Every garden differs, because soil, water, sun exposure, and temperature all play into encouraging or discouraging plants. Your rampaging beast may well be a cosseted treasure in my garden. But no matter how much we enjoy a plant, if growing it has repercussions for our neighbors and surrounding natural areas, it's time to ban that plant.

Bear in mind that gardens have been called staging areas for future invasives. We care for plants, irrigate and fertilize them, plump them up so birds begin to notice and recognize them as food sources. This is why we all need to pay attention and think beyond just what works for us in our own gardens. Just to complicate it further, many invaders have a "lag phase" that can last up to a decade. Sometimes pollinators haven't shown up yet, or it can take a while for birds to recognize fruit on a plant that's new to them.

If all this seems a bit confusing, it is, for the science of invasion biology is only a couple of decades old. A few years ago, a national conference at the Missouri Botanical Garden produced voluntary codes of conduct, or guidelines, to help the gardening public make ethical choices on invasives and potential invasives. See this chapter's "Resources" for more details.

Here are some things every gardener can do to make sure he or she isn't contributing to plant invasions:

- Buy plants from reputable nurseries and catalogs you know and trust.
- Keep a close eye on plants with taproots so deep they're almost impossible to pull out, ones that spread so quickly and efficiently they swamp other plants, or ones that self-seed so vigorously that they colonize an entire bed or border. These are potential bad actors.
- Pay attention to your state's noxious weed list and make sure you never let any plant so designated grow in your garden.

While invasive plants are a global problem, the particular plants that cause these problems can only be determined locally, because a plant's abilities and inclinations toward aggressiveness depend on the conditions in which it grows. So check into local invasive species lists, as well as the Web pages mentioned in this chapter's "Resources" to keep track of which plants cause problems where you live.

Self-Seeders: Nature's Hand in Garden Making

Plants reproduce without any help from humans. Flora creeps, colonizes, and spreads seeds about widely to cover the earth, aided by insects, bees, birds, and butterflies. So we have weeds but also the joy of self-seeding flowers popping up in patterns and combinations more inspired than any we could have figured out ourselves. This life force, this indiscriminate spreading about of plants, is one of the great joys and frustrations of gardening.

Encouraging self-seeders and letting them do what they will feels like joining in partnership with Mother Nature. It's also a smart time- and money-saving strategy for garden making. Self-seeders plump out our gardens and keep us supplied with free plants. In her fine book *A Gentle Plea for Chaos*, Mirabel Osler wrote, "What I like about gardening is that it makes a mockery of intentions." If we can get over our own intentions and accept nature's generosity, we'll learn valuable lessons in how to arrange plants in pleasing patterns.

It's amazing how often self-seeders seem to show up in just the perfect place, adding color to a dull scheme or fluffing up a bed of spindly plants. They fill in, sometimes crowd, adding a casual cottage-garden feel to even the most rigid of plantings. Self-seeders soften the edges. All you need do is edit.

Love-in-a-mist

Honeywort

Flowering tobacco

MODEST BUT RELIABLE SELF-SEEDERS

Here are a few plants that tend to self-seed so modestly but reliably you might want to welcome them into your garden. (Caution: depending on conditions, some of these plants can be quite shy while others can become too aggressive.)

Love-in-a-mist (*Nigella damascena*) is an intricate little flower in mostly shades of blue with ferny foliage and fat, striped pods coveted by flower arrangers.

Tall verbena (*Verbena bonariensis*), the queen of the self-seeders, will grow up happily between other plants; it has a little purple flower midsummer to frost.

Honeywort (*Cerinthe major* 'Purpurascens') is one of those plants you need to buy only once, with thick blue leaves and turquoise and dark purple flowers; lovely with pink roses or in pots.

Flowering tobacco (*Nicotiana sylvestris*) is a statuesque and fragrant plant that grows four to five feet high with long, tubular white flowers.

Santa Barbara daisy (*Erigeron karvinskianus*) has low-growing lacy foliage and long-blooming little white flowers.

Wallflower (*Erysimum* 'Bowles' Mauve') is the kind of pretty, dependable long-bloomer I only wish would reseed in my garden.

Euphorbia dulcis 'Chameleon' is a dainty, dark-leaved euphorbia that looks good with many other plants, retaining its distinct coloration all summer long.

Borage (*Borago officinalis*) has starry cobalt-blue edible flours and hairy stems, which adds up to a far prettier plant than it sounds like.

Nasturtiums of any kind, in my experience, seed about willingly but not so aggressively as to be unwanted.

Poppies of any kind, including California poppies, Shirley poppies, and ruffled "bread seed" poppies, are extremely tough and add bright splashes of color over a long period.

To edit effectively, you need to distinguish between seedlings—which are weeds and which are plants you want to keep? Watch carefully as the baby plants develop and look closely at their leaves; it never hurts to find a book with drawings of weeds so you can distinguish as early on as possible which plants you want to encourage and which you want to pull and dispose of.

I have many flowers in my garden that I never planted at all; pink mullein (*Lychnis coronaria*), forget-me-nots, borage, fennel, toadflax (*Linaria* spp.), feverfew. Toadflax I pull out as soon as I see it, while the others are welcome. Then there are the plants friends have given me just one of that I will now have forever, such as purple columbine, Shirley poppies, and love-in-a-mist (*Nigella damascena*).

The gardener has more options than to leave a plant wherever it chooses to sprout or to pull out these uninvited guests. You can also wait until they have developed a bit of root and move them to a better spot.

How can you tell a rewardingly vigorous self-seeder from one that's downright invasive? As suggested in "Flora Non Grata," check your state's noxious weed list; pay close attention to how aggressively any plant spreads in your garden and get rid of any plant that is colonizing so vigorously it makes you nervous. But remember that most plants, no matter how vigorous and successful at reproducing themselves, are not and never will be an ecological problem. Mostly you can relax and enjoy all those free plants Mother Nature sends your way.

CONTEMPORARY NATIVES: DAVID PFEIFFER'S EDGY, LOW-MAINTENANCE PLANTING STYLE

Who would have imagined that the primeval good looks of native plants could not only hold their own with strong contemporary architecture but also enhance it? Environmental landscaping need not be merely serviceable or well intentioned, as proved by a steep-slope garden as dramatic as the house it surrounds above Lake Washington, north of Seattle.

"The house was so architectural and modern, we chose native plantings to ground it and make it look less artificial," says landscape architect David Pfeiffer of the inspired blend of natives and companion plants he used to anchor the home to its very tough site. The homeowner isn't a gardener, and even if she were,

The man-made and the natural blend seamlessly in a landscape where bluestone pavers and stylish pots consort with boulders, stone steps, and native trees and shrubs. Such yin-yang tension adds dynamism to the simplest, most basic garden design.

"What looks new is using a block of color against a textural backdrop. Right now I'm working on an earthworks garden that is modern in its edited, spare, and graphic forms."

—David Pfeiffer, landscape architect

she wouldn't want to have to weed or water on such a steep site. The water and mountain view from her new home is spectacular, but the cost for that view is the challenge right outside her doors.

Pfeiffer's mostly native plant palette makes the precipitous hillside appear almost as if it's been restored to its natural preconstruction state. Massed grasses along with sturdy trees and shrubs hold their own with the home's strong architecture, especially when teamed up with the concrete slabs and big boulders brought in to shape and retain the site. This is eco-friendly design at its best, with plantings so richly textural and site-appropriate you don't even realize there's no lawn and few flowers.

Every inch of bare soil is thickly planted with ferns, mondo grass, and sarcococca, a balance of ornamentals and natives that will grow in so thickly that not a weed can make its way through the foliage. Birds and wildlife have been drawn back to the hillside, which is quickly regaining some of its wild character as multistemmed vine maples (*Acer circinatum*) and prickly Oregon grape (*Mahonia aquifolium*) fill in along the slopes. A little grove of serviceberry (*Amelanchier* ×*grandiflora*) looks as if it might well have always stood right here next to this striking new contemporary home, especially when a flock of chickadees land to gorge themselves on the autumn fruit.

Walkways, terraces, and patios serve the needs of the homeowner as well as they do the topography of the site. This is design with wisdom, rather than dogma, for aesthetics haven't suffered despite the emphasis on biodiversity and restoration.

The vibe is low-maintenance natural beauty with an edge. The visual pyrotechnics of black bamboo underplanted with chartreuse moss, or silvery eucalyptus growing up to screen out the neighbors, are moderated by the quieter native plantings foaming up quietly around boulders and clothing the slope in green. Plantings around the terrace are native salal (*Gaultheria shallon*), Oregon grape, and strawberry tree (*Arbutus unedo*), yet pleasure was taken into account as well. A hedge of supremely fragrant *Daphne odora* skirts the patio, planted where its scent will waft in through open windows.

"I composed the landscape, placing each plant," says Pfeiffer. Even the trail down to the water was orchestrated so that native thimbleberries, maples, and hemlocks blend gradually and naturally into the surrounding forest.

A strongly designed garden ties the dramatic architecture of the house to its site. The owner isn't a gardener so especially appreciates her low-maintenance landscape that looks anything but.

The terrace is as strong and elemental as the home's modern architecture, paved in slabs of bluestone with cutouts for boulders and ground covers.

In a remodel that transformed a dilapidated cabin into a cool modern house, old wooden decks were replaced with cast iron welding tables salvaged from a local shipyard. Their hunky profile and perforated grid pattern make for surprisingly handsome and weatherproof porches.

Repurposed Materials

Shirley Watts, whose work has been called "foraged urban archeology," is an unrepentant salvage queen. "Don't say recycled materials—it sounds like something you put out on the curb to be picked up," says the modernist San Francisco Bay Area designer. She prefers the term *repurposed* to describe the materials to which she gives new life. Whether old metal numbers, cut concrete, or tumbled dish shards used to cover the ground, these materials are not only earth-friendly but also lend a sense of history, age, and uniqueness to the gardens she designs.

Where better to show our concern for the future of our planet than in our gardens? In the pantheon of sustainable gardening practices, putting old doors, windows, cobbles, bricks, glass, and rusty metal to good use is as vital to the health of the planet as building soil, planting natives, and minimizing lawns.

Many inspiring materials can be found as give-aways at construction sites. Most cities have salvage stores and warehouses of used building products, as well as recycling centers. Then there are the treasure troves of eBay and craigslist. Whether you're looking for an old stove to use as a potting bench, rusty tools to

The skeleton of an iconic womb chair finds second life as a planter holding a *Ranunculus lyallii*.

Richlite, a material made partially of recycled paper and usually used as countertops, moves outdoors to define curvaceous terraces. Designers Glenn Withey and Charles Price chose Richlite for its durability and because it was less expensive than metal.

"Modern is having fun using materials in new ways. Repurposing material is all about history, using something old and giving it a new twist. I don't consider myself a modernist—if you go too geometric you can just kill the space. I love to work with the history of a place and a client's own personal history."

–Shirley Watts,
garden designer

"New is the acceptance of using recycled materials for various structural elements; using better designed products that reduce overall consumption; and incorporating native plants within the overall landscape. However, using only native plants and being smug about it is a complete bore and a turnoff."

−Glenn Withey and Charles Price, garden designers

Nepalese screens are repurposed as garden art, lending height, focal points, and an air of exotica to this otherwise quiet garden.

use as garden art, or a wood-framed window to define a garden space, you can find these and much more by searching online as well as on foot.

And there's no compromise or sacrifice involved in using repurposed materials, for they add patina to a project, as well as interest and individualism. Searching for just the right found object or material helps to cut down on the sheer amount of things used, and using less of everything is the ultimate in going green.

HISTORY-RICH MODERN GARDENS: THE STYLISH DESIGNS OF SHIRLEY WATTS

"I don't consider myself a modernist," says San Francisco Bay Area designer and contractor Shirley Watts. "I love to work with history—the history of a place, or my clients' own personal history." To this end, she uses repurposed materials like

Shirley Watts concocts an inspired mix of the new and old, the modern and the historic in the Smith's courtyard garden in Berkeley.

old signs, tumbled porcelain shards, and metal letters dug out of a salvage bin, even old billboards and computer motherboards, not only for environmental reasons but also to bring meaning and beauty to the gardens she designs.

Her earth-friendly aesthetic extends to plant choice. "I stay away from flashy plants that won't last," says Watts. "I try to make gardens that will endure." She passes up new and trendy plants, and especially perennials, in favor of shrubs and ornamental grasses. And she uses her own garden as a test plot. "If plants survive the minimal care I give them at home, I know I can use them in clients' gardens," says Watts. She laughs when she explains, "I salvaged a boxwood from a dumpster where it had been sitting for a week. I planted it and it survived, so now I use lots of boxwood in my designs."

Perhaps Watts's designs are so compellingly themselves, so charmingly all-of-a-piece, because they're more about her clients' interests and aesthetics than about structures, plants, or a fixed design credo. "There's a certain kind of formulaic modern garden with strict geometry that doesn't work for me," says Shirley. "If you go too geometric you can just kill the space." Yet she anchors the gardens she designs with strong, bold shapes, like the raised rectangular beds and definitive cobalt blue cabana in the Pleasures' garden and the oversized, semicircular aluminum bench in the Smiths' Rose Street garden.

A gravel-like ground cover of tumbled old porcelain dishes (above) brings history and patterning to this very cool modern garden.

THE PLEASURE GARDEN The eye-catching cabanalike structure is an open-air room that divides up a long, narrow urban garden while offering shelter from the cool, foggy San Francisco weather. The structure really deserves a name all its own, for you've never seen anything quite like it. It's glowingly, gleamingly blue, with translucent panels made of polycarbonate that slide like shoji screens to adjust for breeze and temperature. And yet this focal point of the garden is also art, with silk roses encased between its sandwichlike blue panels. The frame is made of durable aluminum, one of Shirley's favorite materials because it weathers well and is endlessly recyclable.

The busy Pleasure family, consisting of two daughters, a neuroscientist father, and a lawyer-MD mother "aren't big gardeners," says Shirley, so part of her task was to create a space that was easy to care for. Shirley began by breaking up the enormous old concrete patio that dominated the narrow twenty-five-by-sixty-three-foot backyard. Then she sliced the concrete into eighteen-inch-wide hunks of various lengths and used it to regrade the garden to drain away from the house and for steps and raised planters. The floor of the garden is pleasantly patterned and crunchy, with tumbled porcelain laid over a couple of inches of base rock. Look closely underfoot to see colors and patterns on the broken-up old thrift-store dishes, speaking of the family's love for collecting pottery. "It's a repurposed material that's hard and strong," says Shirley. "Sifting through it is kind of like finding cool stuff at the beach."

Even the water feature is easy-care, even though anything involving water in a garden is notoriously labor-intensive. Shirley says of the simple rectangular concrete pool with a blue-and-white-patterned urn as focal point, "If you keep the pump running on a regular basis, it stays clean." Recirculating water runs up through the urn, is filtered by the mass of green plants on top, and drips down, making sweet water music while it waters the plants. And birds love the constant drip, the motion, the glistening wet mass of plants atop the urn.

While the furniture is cool and modern (custom-made or purchased from Design Within Reach) as befits this avant-garde space, the plants are tough, durable, and mostly familiar. The concrete-edged beds keep a clean edge on the garden, limiting plantings to a few easy-care groupings. Bamboo, iceberg roses, and wingthorn rose (*Rosa sericea*, grown for its blood-red thorns rather than flowers)

Silver-leafed senecio echoes the silver leaf Shirley applied to this urn, which was filled with gravel and then topped with recycled glass. Water bubbles up and drips down the sides of the pot, much to the delight of the many birds that flock to the Berkeley courtyard garden.

edged with rows of boxwood and masses of auburn *Carex testacea* form the simple yet effective plant palette that plays off the pale pottery shards underfoot and the focal point blue of the cabana.

THE SMITH GARDEN "I love text in gardens," says Shirley Watts of the urban archeology finds she used to turn a little Berkeley courtyard into a history-rich

The Rose Grocery sign, turned into a gate, is left over from the building's decades as a neighborhood grocery store; the stone paving and glass-topped bubbling urn lend a contemporary edge not dependent on plants or upkeep for impact.

garden. In a former reincarnation, the building was the Rose Grocery for thirty years. But it had been abandoned and fallen into ruin until a young architect clever enough to save the old façade turned it into a duplex. Now the old bakery sign serves as a garden door, bringing words, color, and texture as well as a reminder of earlier days to the little garden.

The courtyard is an essential part of the house, for the living room is on one side and owner Patricia Smith's quilting studio is on the other. Paved and planted, with big metal letters Shirley scavenged from a local salvage yard embedded here and there in the flooring, the courtyard space reads like another room, albeit open air.

Patricia is an avid gardener, so Shirley left plenty of space for her to plant bulbs and other favorite plants. But she took care to give the garden an urban edge with bold design elements, like the thirteen-foot-wide semicircular aluminum bench that defines the space and edges a bed with its swoop and shine while serving as seating for guests and parties. "It sets up a geometry," says Shirley. "Scale is so important in small gardens; larger things have such great impact."

The bench's considerable presence is balanced by a generous S-curved bed planted in a mass of 'Karl Foerster' feather reed grass (*Calamagrostis ×acutiflora*), punctuated by a willowy, swaying wind sculpture made of aluminum. "It's a simple setup," says Shirley of the vertical strips of aluminum, "but it's very effective because they move and cast shadows."

Then there's the concrete urn filled with recycled glass, which must be the ultimate in low-maintenance pots. Shirley silver-leafed the urn, piped it so that water bubbles up through the glass, and planted black mondo grass and spiky little *Phormium* 'Jack Spratt' at its feet. The effect is simple and dramatic, and the birds flock to the dripping water. "We just left it without plants," says Shirley. "We decided we liked it plain like that" in a bold stroke that eliminated all maintenance yet created a stunning focal point.

Climateproofing Your Garden

There's been a lot of buzz about climate change. What does it really mean for gardeners? Gardeners are connoisseurs of weather, closely attuned to every variable, which puts us on the front lines of dealing with changing weather patterns. You've probably already noticed changes like later-blooming plants or more pests.

Repurposed metal letters, unearthed by designer Shirley Watts at a salvage store, give character and dimension to the paving in this courtyard garden.

Designer Shirley Watts makes the most of small spaces; a narrow strip of planting bed against the court-yard wall holds not just the focal-point shiny wands of aluminum wind sculpture but also fluffs of ornamental grasses and flowering perennials, accented by a fat bowl of succulents.

"I consider every plant hardy until I have killed it myself . . . at least three times," says Tony Avent, owner of Plant Delights Nursery. He and all the rest of us aren't killing off as many plants these days, for one reality of global warming is that plants we used to consider borderline are fully hardy. How many plants in your garden would not have weathered winter even just a few years ago?

International scientists agree that the earth's average annual temperature is rising and that this global warming is a result of human activity. Depending on location, these climatic changes may show up as more frequent and intense storms, extended droughts, higher temperatures, shifts in the timing of the seasons, and erratic, unpredictable weather. This means that changing weather patterns are already seriously and confusingly affecting our plants and gardens.

The National Wildlife Federation has published a forward-thinking and useful little book called *The Gardener's Guide to Global Warming: Challenges and Solutions*. The NWF understands that while climate change is global, its affects are as local as our backyards. Birds are migrating earlier each spring, and lilacs are flowering two weeks earlier than they did just thirty years ago.

I spoke with Patty Glick, editor of *The Gardener's Guide*, about what further changes gardeners should brace for. She expects that weather will only grow more extreme and unpredictable. Expect less snowpack, drier summers, wetter winters. Plants are stressed by these extremes so become more susceptible to insects and disease. And these pests will be ever more troublesome, taking full advantage of warmer temperatures to increase their ranges and virulence. Lest we get too discouraged, Glick reminds us that nature is enormously resilient if we work with natural systems rather than run roughshod over them.

As gardeners we can make a difference, for how we collectively garden has planetary impact. Here are a few ideas to help gardeners adapt to climate change as well as do our part to help prevent it:

SOIL AND COMPOST

- Healthy, compost-enriched soil is better at absorbing water and provides the foundation for thriving plants that are more resistant to disease, drought, or insect damage. Healthy soil stores carbon from the atmosphere, helping to reduce greenhouse gases. It also has less need for fertilizers or pesticides (the production of which generates greenhouse gases). Composting your yard waste and food scraps keeps them out of the landfill, where organic materials create methane, a very potent greenhouse gas.

PLANTS

- Choose tough, sturdy, self-reliant plants suited to your garden's climate and conditions, so that they'll need less water and fertilizer, and thrive with as little intervention from you as possible. Healthy plants are naturally resistant to pests and diseases.

WATER

- Reduce water consumption with drought-tolerant and native plants.
- Group plants with like water needs to cut down on the overall use of water in the garden.
- Irrigate with drip systems or soaker hoses; adjust watering to soil, weather, and seasonal conditions; and use tools like watering bags to keep new trees healthy. Remember to check whether your soil is dry before watering, and make sure you're watering more than just the surface.

Rainfall management is turned into a design feature in this Bainbridge Island garden. Rainwater cascades off the roof to flow down this heavy linked rain chain into a stone-filled pot.

- Global warming is creating what climatologists call "heavier rainfall events." This means more runoff and more storm water problems, flooding, and pollution in our creeks, rivers, and lakes. This problem can be largely solved in our own gardens by avoiding chemical fertilizers, pesticides, and herbicides, and

" Today's broad interest in sustainability renews the importance of no-fuss landscape plants. Plantings in the truly modern garden are tough enough to withstand a changing global climate."

—Scot Medbury, president and CEO of Brooklyn Botanic Garden

During winter storms, rainwater is channeled through this low-lying, boulder-strewn channel. In drier seasons of the year, the dry streambed is a design feature, especially in May when purple *Allium giganteum* outline its banks.

by using porous surfaces like pebbles, gravels, or pavers rather than solid concrete for patios and driveways. Install rain barrels and cisterns to capture rainwater to use for irrigation. Consider taking advantage of low-lying or boggy spots in your garden to create a rain garden, planted with moisture-loving natives, to slow down the passage of rainwater through the soil.

CREATURES

- As climate change drives ecosystems out of sync, pollinators are decoupled from plants. Gardeners can help by planting a diverse array of blooming plants that flower both early and late.
- Help birds, bees, and insects weather climate change by nurturing them in your garden, which means eschewing all chemicals. Plant natives that have evolved along with the flora, and plenty of berried plants to feed and attract creatures.

TOOLS AND PRACTICES

- Use solar lights wherever possible and cut energy usage for all other outdoor lights by putting them on a timer.
- Get rid of your gas mower. According to Glick, gas mowers are so inefficient that running one for an hour generates as much pollution as idling forty late-model cars for the same length of time. If you can't bear to part with your lawn, use a hand or electric mower. And choose rakes and hand clippers over gasoline-powered tools like weed eaters and leaf blowers, for blessed quiet as well as energy efficiencies.

Top Ten Gardening Tips to Save the Planet

Millions around the world garden—which means that if each of us steps up to be stewards of the earth as well as our own little plots, we can make a huge difference in the quality of life on earth.

1. **Get rid of your lawn.** The U.S. Environmental Protection Agency calculates that fifty-four million Americans mow their lawns every week. Think of the gas used, the fumes, and the noise, let alone the water and fertilizer it took to grow those lawns. Tear it out and replace it with less thirsty eco-lawn, edibles, ground covers, or other permeable surfaces.

2. **Banish pesticides and herbicides.** Beneficial insects are killed, soil is sterilized, fish are slaughtered by toxic runoff, and our own health is endangered by our addiction to the easy fix of using poisons in our gardens. And here's the irony—you don't need them to grow a beautiful garden.

3. **Conserve water.** Use a rain barrel to harvest water off the roof to water your plants, save water in cisterns to meet summer irrigation needs, fix leaky faucets, improve the soil, group thirsty plants together, and water only as often and as much as you need to.

4. **Apply compost and mulch.** These are the wonder drugs of the garden, for nothing else enriches and improves soil, prevents water evaporation, and creates a healthy growing environment for plants like the regular application of compost and mulch.

5. **Put the right plant in the right place.** Site plants with thought, giving them the sun, shade, and soil they need to thrive with less intervention from you.

6. **Plant natives.** Adding even a few native plants to your garden, if properly placed to give them the conditions they prefer, cuts down on work and resources while providing habitat and food for birds, bees, and butterflies.

7. **Banish invasives.** Keep tabs on your state and county invasive plant list to make sure you aren't growing plants that escape beyond the garden gate to wreak havoc in parks and wildlands.

8. **Reuse, repurpose, recycle.** Nature is the ultimate recycler, turning fallen leaves and dying plants into compost to build the soil. Follow nature's lead and compost yard waste and kitchen scraps. Build garden infrastructure with repurposed or recycled materials whenever possible. Buy plants in biodegradable pots, find local nurseries that will recycle plastic pots, or turn them into garden art.

9. **Buy and grow local.** You can't eat any more locally than what you pick right outside your own door, so dedicate some garden space to growing food for your family. Even planting a few berries, lettuces, tomatoes, and herbs in pots, the ground, or raised beds can help you eat fresh and cut down on grocery bills, as well as giving you the satisfaction of growing your own. Buy plants at local nurseries rather than by mail order whenever possible.

10. **Garden with a light hand.** Less pruning, less watering, less fertilizing, less manipulation of the garden uses fewer resources and creates less waste. Learning to tolerate less than perfection and cultivating restraint help. Building and planting thoughtfully with quality materials and plants you love that are well suited to your garden's conditions means that the garden will last, in no small part because you won't want to continually change it. Observe the weather, your plants, and the changing seasons, and intervene only when necessary.

Hummingbirds are drawn to red flowers; here a hummer sups on the extravagant midsummer blooms of devil's tobacco (*Lobelia tupa*).

WEATHER AND MICROCLIMATES

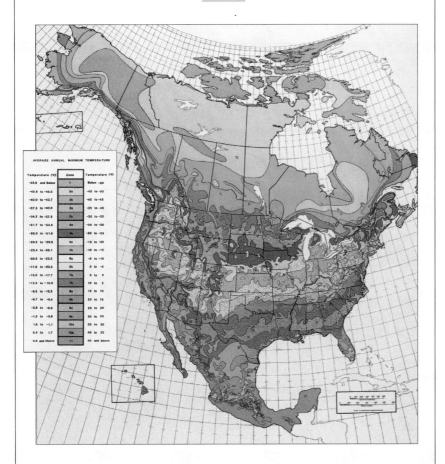

USDA plant hardiness zone map

I've never met a gardener who doesn't love to talk about the weather. If you're ever wondering how low the temperature dropped or how much it rained when you were away from home, ask a gardener and you'll learn the exact details, as well as stories about how that compares with previous years' weather on the same date.

Weather intrigues because it's ever changing and often surprising (even before global warming). Even freeze damage isn't an absolute but depends on timing. A sharp freeze in November may kill off a slew of borderline plants, while several days of the same temperatures in January, once plants have hardened off, cause less devastation.

Then there's the USDA plant hardiness zone map, which can be helpful but also limiting. I've met people who say things like "I can't grow banana trees because I'm a zone 7" as if that number was stamped on their fore-head. If they found a protected spot in their garden, warm with sun reflected off a wall, and wrapped the tree in winter, perhaps they could grow a banana tree. And if they really love banana trees, it may be worth all the work.

Often drought-loving plants like rosemary or lavender don't make it through the winter not because of a drop in temperature but because their roots rot. Improving drainage helps many plants live through cold weather. So take this map as a rough guideline for which plants do best where you live. You'll learn much more about what will work in your own garden by carefully observing conditions, talking with other gardeners in your area, and visiting local public gardens and arboreta. And you'll learn best through experimenting, killing off a few plants, and nurturing others along.

And then there is the mystery of microclimates, for each of our gardens has its own pockets of warmth, cold, drought, and damp. You may be able to grow a fig tree against a south-facing wall even if you live in zone 6 or 7, or winter over semi-tender tropicals in zone 8 if you provide a warm, sheltered spot for them.

Even within a small geographic area, temperatures and growing condi-tions vary considerably depending on your garden's elevation, frost pock-ets, and how the winds blow through and the sun hits. Placement of the house on the property, fences, walls, and paving all create and influence microclimates. Perhaps in your back garden, tomatoes stay green into September, but you might be able to ripen them if you grow them in pots along the sidewalk where they'd bask in reflected heat. Get to know the microclimates in your garden to take advantage of the many opportunities they offer.

In well-drained soil, in climates where freezes are rare, no ground covers are more showy and easy care than a medley of succulents in contrasting shapes and colors.

Feverfew (*Tanacetum parthenium*) is a long bloomer that readily self-seeds without taking over. Here feverfew's daisylike flowers mingle in a cheerful haze with herbs and other perennials.

Keep It Simple

- Choose plants that last. San Francisco Bay Area designer Shirley Watts uses durable, long-lived plants in her landscapes, choosing shrubs and trees over perennials, both for easy care and a landscape that doesn't generate so much waste and black plastic pots left over from changing out plantings. "I try to design gardens that will endure," says Watts, and this philosophy extends to plants as well as materials.

- Look to creative repurposing as an inexpensive and fun source of garden materials that add instant history and patina to the garden. Old faucets work as water features, doorknobs as hose guides or to add texture and interest to walls or screens. Recycled wood and rusty metal age and mellow a new garden, while crushed and tumbled pottery used to cover the ground is permeable and pretty. Concrete pads, patios, and driveways can be broken up or cut and used as retaining walls, pavers, and to build raised beds. Old gates, doors, and windows can be reused in the garden for their original purpose or fashioned into outdoor tables or screens. Salvage stores, building sites, and building supply stores are all sources of used materials.

- Rainwater is free—and it runs right off your roof into the ground and storm drains, causing problems during storms and not helping a bit to irrigate your garden. Whether you dangle an elegant rain chain into a rain barrel and water your pots with what you collect, or set up a cistern and storage tank system to harvest every drop that falls on your roof, rainwater is yours to use and to save until you need it. (Check your local municipalities regulations on downspouts and rainwater collection.)

- Encourage self-seeders. Nature provides plenty of free plants, their seeds distributed by the wind, insects, and birds. Often these plants fill in bare spots and blend with existing plantings in lovely, educative ways. Learn to know the difference between weedy and desirable seedlings and pay attention to your state's noxious weed list so you don't harbor dangerously aggressive plants in your garden. But mostly enjoy what nature provides, learn from the patterns self-seeders create, or move them about the garden to suit your own planting schemes.

A barrel hooked up to a downspout and outfitted with a faucet is a simple and inexpensive way to harvest rainwater off the roof to use when and where needed in the garden.

Resources

BOOKS   *Bringing Nature Home: How You Can Sustain Wildlife with Native Plants*, revised and expanded, by Douglas W. Tallamy (Timber Press, 2009). How rarely scientists write books gardeners can understand! Tallamy, professor of entomology and wildlife ecology, is the exception. He writes convincingly and practically about the complex ecological web that supports and sustains creatures, and how we can play our parts by growing a diversity of native plants in our backyards.

The Gardener's Guide to Global Warming: Challenges and Solutions by Patty Glick (National Wildlife Federation, 2007). The report is available for download at www.nwf.org/gardenersguide/. Everything a gardener needs to know about how to prepare your garden for the realities of global warming, as well as how to do your part to prevent it.

A Gentle Plea for Chaos by Mirabel Osler (Arcade Publishing, 1998). Perfectionists beware. This classic of garden literature makes the case for taking our cues from nature, letting up a bit, and enjoying our gardens more.

The Green Gardener's Guide: Simple, Significant Actions to Protect and Preserve Our Planet by Joe Lamp'l (Cool Springs Press, 2007). This straightforward book brings tried-and-true organic gardening techniques into the new millennium. The author, host of GardenSMART on PBS, has a knack for effective, simple explanations of how individual gardening practices affect your own health and the future of the planet.

Hardy Succulents: Tough Plants for Every Climate by Gwen Moore Kelaidis (Storey, 2008). Succulents are the plants of the future. The hardy ones in this beautifully photographed book are tough and durable enough to take whatever climate change throws at them.

Right Plant, Right Place: Over 1,400 Plants for Every Situation in the Garden, revised and updated, by Nicola Ferguson (Fireside Books, 2005). This is the handbook that will help you realize the goal of choosing just the right plants for the conditions that exist in your own garden. Whether you're looking for green flowers, bronze foliage, or plants tolerant of dense shade or clay soil (or both), you'll find extensive lists and hundreds of color photos to guide you.

Wabi Sabi: The Japanese Art of Impermanence by Andrew Juniper (Tuttle, 2003). This modest little book is one of the few intelligible ones I've ever found on the elusive concept of wabi sabi. It gently and persuasively convinces that imperfection, impermanence, decline, and decay aren't problems but an ancient art form well suited to gardening in tune with nature.

The Wild Braid: A Poet Reflects on a Century in the Garden by Stanley Kunitz, with Genine Lentine (Norton, 2005). How better to gain a deeper understanding of nature's mysteries than through the words of one of our greatest poets? In this series of remarkable conversations with Stanley Kunitz, you learn how his seaside garden has served as solace, renewal, and muse over his long lifetime. He understands and loves nature's cycles and rhythms, and his appreciation of her wonders shines through his words, poems, and the touching photos of Kunitz enjoying his garden in his hundredth year.

ONLINE RESOURCES   **Canadian Recycled Plastic Products**, www.crplastics.com. The Generation Line of garden furniture is not only durable and weatherproof but also made of material destined for landfills.

The Center for Plant Conservation publishes its voluntary codes of conduct for the gardening public at www.centerforplantconservation.org/invasives/gardeningN.html.

Durable Plastic Design, www.orcaboard.com. Check out this site for outdoor chairs and planters made of recycled milk jugs.

Environment and Human Health, Inc., www.ehhi.org, is an organization of doctors, public health professionals, and policy experts committed to reducing environmental health risks to individuals.

The Global Invasive Species Database, www.invasives.org, can be searched by habitat, country, or type of organism, plant, or animal. The taxonomy is current, and the scope impressive.

The National Invasive Species Information Center, www.invasivespeciesinfo.gov. Despite its consideration of natives down to the level of microbes, this U.S. Department of Agriculture site is user friendly, with current information on community action and suggestions on what each of us can do to protect the health of our environment.

The Rain Garden Network, www.raingardennetwork.com, is a community of people and organizations promoting a new approach to water management. This site is geared to the home gardener. Learn what, who, how, and why, beginning with the comforting stance that "rain gardens don't need to be large or complicated."

Rosalind Creasy's garden is where the food-in-your-front-yard revolution started more than thirty years ago. A colorful wall and gate, a brick path, and stepping-stones give an edge to the vegetables, herbs, and edible flowers flourishing streetside.

Eat Your Garden

GROWING OUR OWN FOOD IS NOTHING NEW, despite its resurgence as a driving force in home gardening. After all, planting seeds, tending the soil, and harvesting crops moved people past their nomadic ways and into a more civilized phase of human history.

In our hectic, sometimes dangerous, and often confusing world, growing our own food once again feels civilizing. Planting herbs, vegetables, and fruit ties us to the soil and nature's rhythms while assuring a safe and healthy source of fresh food. Nurseries are selling fewer ornamental plants, but in the spring of 2008 sales of vegetable seeds and starts were up fivefold over the previous year, and 39 percent of the people surveyed by the Garden Writers Association said they'd be growing vegetables, up from 32 percent in the spring of 2007.

Few things we turn our time and talents to are as deliciously gratifying as picking a sun-warmed raspberry or cherry tomato and popping it into our mouths, snipping cilantro or chives to spark a dish, or feasting on sweet corn we've picked minutes before it hits the boiling water.

ABOVE: Pumpkins, like this French heirloom 'Cinderella', are gratifying to grow as they fatten and color up over the summer, coming into their own as the garden dies down in October.

OPPOSITE: A rusted steel spiral of a raised bed holds an entire season's worth of healthy, delicious lettuces and herbs.

Young people have grown up with organics, farmers' markets, and CSAs (community supported agriculture farms), which is why they put such a high value on safe, fresh food that they're devoting much of their precious outdoor space to growing it. As we pay more for our little bits of real estate, we pay greater attention to how we use our outdoor spaces. For generations X and Y, space for outdoor dining

Contained by a picket fence, showy 'Gold Rush' zucchini sprawl comfortably in Ros Creasy's productive front garden, where marigolds brighten the scene while repelling insects.

and entertaining competes with growing food in pots, window boxes, and every inch of available soil. Even seasoned ornamental gardeners like me, who grew up on frozen and canned vegetables, are devoting more and more garden space to edibles.

Rosalind Creasy led the way with her quite literally ground-breaking volume *The Complete Book of Edible Landscaping*, published in 1982. Her brave foray into planting basil and peppers, then tomatoes and strawberries, in front of her California home revolutionized our understanding of how beautiful vegetables can be. Her back garden was too shady, so she asked the obvious questions: Why not turn a sterile, sun-drenched sweep of lawn into a productive vegetable plot? Why not grow edibles ornamentally?

While Creasy's fresh take on edibles may have shocked the neighbors, it sprung vegetables loose from their traditional neat rows and designated plots. And they've never returned to such arbitrary confinement, in either our gardens or our minds.

Gardeners around the country now enjoy fruit and vegetables for their visuals as well as their taste and nutrition. As a result, breeders have worked to produce more compact, ruffled, striped, colorful, and otherwise attractive vegetables, helping to fulfill Creasy's vision of beautiful front yard vegetable gardening.

Vegetable Politics

What for Creasy was personal, sparked by her own gardening and cooking, has become political thanks to a new generation of vegetable activists. Fritz Haeg, a young Los Angeles architect, questions the sanity of Americans' love affair with their front lawns in his manifesto of a book, *Edible Estates: Attack on the Front Lawn*. "The front lawn was born of vanity and decadence, under the assumption that fertile land was infinite," he writes. We can no longer afford such illusions, especially when we need look no farther than just outside our own front and back doors for a spot to grow our own sumptuous harvest.

Haeg suggests that we respond to today's overload of planetary challenges by creating an organic, productive, delicious, and beautiful world in our own gardens—the kind of world in which we want to live. Rather than feel helpless in the face of climate change, pollution, overcrowding, crime, etcetera, etcetera, he suggests we get busy ripping out grass, improving the soil, and growing food.

Translucent, floral-scented gooseberries are as lovely growing in the garden as they are delicious eaten fresh or cooked into a pie, fool, or crumble.

Roger Doiron, founder of Kitchen Gardens International, takes Haeg's manifesto a step farther. With all the bravado that comes from creating a virtual community of 5200 gardeners from ninety-six different countries, Doiron is advocating an edible landscape at the White House. He wants carrots and broccoli growing in front of the White House as a lesson on saving energy for all Americans. His reasoning? It takes ten calories of fossil fuel to produce every single calorie of food consumed. This is because the average food item in the United States travels fifteen hundred miles from field to fork, meaning it costs four hundred gallons of fuel. What lunacy! How did we get into this fix, when most of us have soil right outside our back doors, or community gardens (called P-patches in Seattle) within walking distance?

Doiron dug up his own front lawn, in front his family's "white house" in Maine, replacing it with a vegetable plot. The edible-izing of his front garden is captured in the mock-stirring video "This Lawn Is Your Lawn," a hit on YouTube. Eat the View is the name of the energetic Doiron's campaign to plant healthy, edible landscapes in high-impact, high-visibility places around the country, starting with, he hopes, the White House. Why mow when you can harvest?

It's not like growing beets and rutabagas at the highest levels of government is unprecedented. Eleanor Roosevelt's own victory garden at the White House inspired millions around the United States to use their home landscapes to grow food, as is Michelle Obama's garden today. At the peak of the victory garden enthusiasm, Americans grew 40 percent of the nation's fruit and vegetables. As Thomas Jefferson, that great gardener and nature enthusiast, said, "Cultivators of the earth are the most valuable citizens."

A Personal Take

But for most of us, what we choose to grow in our gardens remains intensely personal. Despite gardening most of my life, until the last few years I'd never grown vegetables except for a token tomato or two in a pot, and always a pumpkin vine if I could spare the space. I couldn't bear to give up a single perennial, rose, or shrub to ground-gobbling squashes, let alone all the staking, trellising, and sequencing involved in growing edibles. But all that changed when I downsized my garden, in part because I was looking for a new gardening challenge. And I was inspired by my young adult children's interest in fresh vegetables, herbs, and cooking from the garden.

Everbearing strawberries 'Tristar' cascade down the side of a metal feed trough where they ripen quickly in the heat reflected off the gravel and the trough. I trim most of the beds in my garden with strawberries, yielding enough fruit for breakfast or dessert through most of the summer months.

In my new small garden there's no room for a hidden-away vegetable patch that looks bleak part of the year. The edibles needed to hold their own visually. So I started looking for models. Impressive French and Italian potagers feature the right mix of ornamental and edible but are too formal and labor intensive. I found inspiration in the gardens of artist Johanna Nitzke Marquis and landscape architect David Pfeiffer, which you'll get a glimpse of later in this chapter. Both loosely and artistically combine flowers, herbs, fruits, lettuces, and vegetables in raised beds. Their gardens are as gorgeous as they are productive.

So now I mostly have raised beds and pots, planted in an overblown, colorful mix of flowers and vegetables and herbs. The hard edges of the beds bring symmetry and discipline to the scene, the plants are easier to reach, the soil is better, and the plants are protected (somewhat) from slugs, snails, and a rambunctious puppy. I grow a row of raspberries right down the center of one of the raised boxes, surrounded by aggressive flowers like love-in-a-mist and California poppies that hold their own with the raspberries. A neat edging of Spanish lavender brings a little order to that bed. Round galvanized feed troughs are centered with a bay tree, dwarf pole apple, and tomatoes, and each is trimmed out with strawberries, pumpkins, and nasturtiums.

Choosing which edibles are worth growing in such restricted space is a challenge. And I thought it was hard to select just a few hydrangeas, a single rose, one color of poppy! That's nothing compared to salivating over the Raintree or Nichols Garden Nursery catalog and having to reject juicy heirloom tomatoes and chocolate mint. Here's the drill: Which ones will we most enjoy eating, which are beautiful, what kinds can be eliminated because they're readily available at the local farmers' market? I've found lettuces, berries, tomatoes, and herbs to be the most rewarding. Also pumpkins and pea pods and arugula.

Perhaps the most important criterion is simply how easy any veggie is to grow, for we won't be successful with plants that seem more trouble than they're worth. Veggies and herbs peak quickly, flop, bolt, need more space than you'd ever imagine, and require supports, irrigation, regular picking, fertilizing, and rotations. Bugs love them. Part of the trick is to expand your notion of ornamental. I love the edible pea pods I'm growing this summer, even though they've wildly outgrown the ornamental cages I'd so naively planted them in. One is prettily

Thyme, zucchini, and 'Red Giant' Japanese mustard mingle together in a colorful, textural summer display, as delicious as it is ornamental.

" The best modern gardeners are people who work joyfully together to create beauty and food and alter the way we live. They can imagine the future."

–Jason Dewees, horticulturist and palm broker at Flora Grubb Gardens, San Francisco

entwined with a stand of alstroemeria, the other has climbed up to colonize a bronze fennel. I've learned to accept such happy coincidences, and next year I'll plant my pea pods against a fence.

I suggest you don't spend too much time thinking about what each bean or tomato actually costs, because in both time and dollars it's probably not an encouraging equation. Growing your own is all about the beauty and sensuality of it, the taste, freshness, and peace of mind that come from harvesting organic veggies out of your own garden.

Remember that vegetables don't acquiesce to crowding like ornamentals do. But it's so worth it. Such a simple pleasure as stepping out the door with colander and scissors in hand to snip lettuces, lemon verbena, basil, and mint never pales. I admire the checkerboard effect of chartreuse and purple lettuces as much as any clematis or lily, and I could never have believed that picking fragrantly ripe strawberries for breakfast is such an entirely different sensory experience from buying them at the store.

Garden Where You Live

All gardening is place-specific—especially edible gardening. Even more than with ornamentals, success with vegetables and fruits depends on your garden's soil and microclimates. Edibles have very specific requirements for sunlight and soil, and they malinger if these aren't met, while succeeding stupendously when they are.

Every good gardener is both detective and careful observer. Begin by noticing where the sun hits your garden, where the frost lingers on cold mornings. Clue in to where the wind whistles through and which parts of the garden are most protected. Microclimates come with the lay of the land and can be influenced by placement of fences, houses, walls, and paving. But only when you understand and accept the reality of where you garden can you effectively play around with microclimates and amend your soil to expand what you can grow well.

Then comes the detective part of the equation, which means tracking down the best gardening information available for your region of the country. A great place to start is the master gardener program for your area, which is sponsored by your state's university or college extension service. Unfortunately, because there's no national oversight for the master gardener program, we lack a consistent, reli-

"Nourishing, fast-growing greens are the future of vegetable gardening because of people's health concerns."

–Rose Marie Nichols McGee, proprietor of Nichols Garden Nursery

able Web site listing all the master gardening programs. The easiest thing to do is simply google "Master Gardeners" along with the name of your county or state to find the program nearest you. Master gardeners produce region-specific, detailed publications, offer free one-on-one advice, and often host a demonstration garden with events like tomato taste-offs and composting classes. Consider taking the training, which is expert and up to date, and requires a payback of volunteering, from which you might learn even more than from the classes.

Local, organic food is a hot topic, and visiting local farmers' markets is a great way to hook into the web of people in your area concerned with fresh food. You'll see arrayed before you the flowers, fruits, and vegetables that grow best and ripen most easily in your region. Often organic starts and seeds are sold at these markets. Ask questions of the farmers and check out the information booths; you'll meet people whose passion and business it is to help you become a more knowledgeable gardener.

Why learn the hard way? Gardening is an art well served by relying on the knowledge and experience of those who have gardened long and hard before you.

Listening to Rosalind Creasy

"Twenty-five years ago heirloom tomatoes were considered crazy, and now Trader Joe's carries blue potatoes!" exclaims Rosalind Creasy, the woman brave enough to spring vegetables out of the patch and into the front yard. Although she revolutionized our thinking about how and where to grow food plants in her 1982 classic *The Complete Book of Edible Landscaping*, Ros modestly claims she was influenced by others. "There was a whole new breed of farmers in California in the late 1970s and early '80s," Ros says, "and I learned so much from the California Rare Fruit Growers and, of course, from Alice Waters." (Waters founded the restaurant Chez Panisse in Berkeley, California, and with it the fresh, local food revolution. Today she's a cookbook author and activist for schoolyard gardens).

So what does the godmother of beautiful veggie gardening, the woman who moved her fruit and veggies out front long before this was a popular or even acceptable idea, recommend for new food gardeners?

"It's easy and effective to plant in whiskey and wine barrels—they're perfect for all vegetables except corn," she says. "The depth is right, they hold enough water, drain well, and the wood doesn't absorb heat." Ros suggests growing an

Edibles like these espaliered lemons are grown ornamentally in Ros Creasy's trend-setting California garden.

Ros cuddling Mr. X, her Silver
Duckwing Old English bantam
known for lording it over the
seven resident hens.

ROS'S PICKS

After thirty years of growing edibles, Ros has thoroughly vetted the field. Here's her list of the most beautiful and best-tasting herbs, fruit, and veggies, all pretty enough to grow in your front garden. (Keep in mind Ros lives and gardens in Los Altos, California, so this is a warm-weather list of plants, although many grow well in a range of climates).

Ruby chard, especially the pinks and whites, which Ros grows with little wave petunias in similar color tones.

'Sweet Baby Girl', a new dwarf cherry tomato with especially sweet fruit on half-sized vines.

Lemon basil, with citrus-scented leaves ideal for grilling or livening up salads and pastas.

Eggplants, especially the daintier, more slender Japanese types. She also favors the heirloom Italian eggplant 'Rosa Bianca', which is mild tasting and teardrop shaped, with gray fuzzy leaves and purple flowers.

Peppers. Ros grows variegated Bolivian peppers with ruffled purple coleus. *Capsicum annuum* 'Super Chili' is fiery hot, while cherry peppers are milder and sweeter.

Artichokes, for their structure and height as well as taste.

'Gold Rush' zucchini, which has big yellow flowers and bright golden yellow fruit, is showy enough all on its own and even more dramatic when complemented with marigolds and nasturtiums.

Dwarf blueberries, which she declares must be on every food gardener's list of favorites.

Strawberries, especially the day-neutral types like 'Seaside' and 'Tristar' (day-neutral strawberries are insensitive to day length and will flower and runner continuously as long as the temperature stays between 35 and 85 degrees F), which in her climate bear fruit for four or five months of the year. Ros grows these to drip down the sides of her streetside retaining wall, where she can share them with the neighborhood.

entire edible garden in a barrel. "You could plant an 'Early Girl' tomato, a couple of pepper plants, a summer squash, and even some edamame in a single barrel and eat from it all summer."

Fill a second barrel with what Ros calls "herbs with training wheels" in a sunny spot right outside your kitchen. Chosen for their ease and dependability, these are also the herbs most useful for cooking: perennial chives, oregano, thyme, sage, parsley, and tarragon. In summer when the soil warms up, stick in some basil, and then plant cilantro in either early spring or autumn to complete your fragrant herb barrel.

In spring, Ros grows a barrel or two of pink tulips, trimmed with ruffled salad mesclun that foams up around the stems of the tulips to make an idyllic picture. "I'm a nut case for baby greens," says Ros. "I never wait for them to mature but clip them as soon as there's anything to cut." Ros always plants plenty of old-fashioned annuals like zinnias, cosmos, and nasturtiums to bloom amidst the vegetables, for color and contrast and because of the beneficial insects attracted to the flowers.

> "A garden is not truly a garden for people unless it has tomatoes."
>
> –Rose Marie Nichols McGee, proprietor of Nichols Garden Nursery

Edibles expert Rose Marie Nichols McGee recommends cherry tomatoes like 'Sun Gold' or these 'Red Pearl' that are sweet and rapid-ripening.

Learning from Rose Marie Nichols McGee

Rose Marie Nichols McGee, co-author of *The Bountiful Container*, influences trends in home gardening from her vantage point as president of Nichols Garden Nursery, a flourishing mail order business that's sold new and unusual herbs, vegetables, and edible flowers nationwide for more than fifty years.

Rose Marie not only sells plants but also gardens extensively at home in Corvallis, Oregon, and at the Albany, Oregon, display gardens of her company. She encourages gardeners not to pass up the newer hybrid seeds and starts in favor of venerable heirlooms. "Breeders have made significant advances in flavor and disease resistance," says McGee, giving the new 'Legend' tomato as an example. This big, early-ripening, full-flavor tomato resists late blight, which gives it a chance to actually ripen in less-than-hot climates or those where fall weather arrives a little too early. "The heirloom buzz is a real thing," says Rose Marie, "but many of the newer varieties are healthier."

This doyenne of edibles started growing veggies and herbs in pots to help out her arthritis-impaired mother. Rose Marie bought her mom some containers so she could dig in the dirt and harvest her own vegetables without kneeling or bending down. So while Rose Marie began growing contained veggies for practi-

Lettuce sprouts from seed planted directly into a thin layer of good soil on top of a hay bale, a new idea for raised beds that provide their own nutrients to grow peppers or lettuces.

ROSE MARIE ON HERBS

"There's no way to get more mileage per square inch than to grow herbs," says Rose Marie. It takes her only a minute to come up with a half-sun, half-shade herb pot combination that will decorate your deck while spicing up your cooking. Here's her recipe for a gratifying pot of herbs:

- one columnar basil
- one variegated sage, which is prettier and not so vigorous as a solid-color-leafed sage and worth growing because fresh sage is so much better than dried
- one rosemary 'Mozart', which is semiprostrate so will drape over the sides of the pot, with beautiful blue flowers
- one Sicilian oregano, which is not too hot and a little sweet, with the best flavor of all the oreganos
- one tarragon, which does best in a pot because it needs good drainage
- one compact 'Fern Leaf' dill plant

TIPS FOR DEALING WITH PROBLEM HERBS:

- Keep mint confined to a pot. Never let it loose in the ground, because it spreads aggressively and is impossible to dig out.
- When parsley gets huge and leggy, just pull it out and start over.
- When you harvest chives, cut each stem down to its base; also cut the stems way down after flowering for a fresh flush of green.

cal reasons, she's pursued it for beauty. Despite owning acres of land, Rose Marie is still experimenting with the tastiest, prettiest edibles that best lend themselves to being grown in what she describes as "small, carefully managed spaces."

Rose Marie is excited about hay bale gardening. "If you want raised beds that heat up faster, or have problem soil, just plant right into a hay bale, which will slowly break down to improve the soil beneath it," she explains. The look may be rustic, but tomatoes, peppers, and lettuces love the nutrients they draw out of the

Old-fashioned pansies and dramatically colored chard are natural companions with their contrasting forms and colors; both perform best in cool weather.

Chive blossoms attract bees, butterflies, and humans with their cheery little lavender flower balls.

hay. Just put a thin layer of good soil on top of the hay bail and plant directly into it, for the simplest, least expensive raised-bed gardening ever.

What's new in the Nichols catalog? Rose Marie recommends the new columnar basil (also called 'Aussie Sweetie') because it doesn't bolt and stays a tidy size and shape ideal for pots and urban gardens. No pinching back all the time as with most basils, because it doesn't flower and it grows about three feet tall and only a foot wide. This is the skinny basil with the big taste, for each leaf bursts with the fragrance and flavor of this favorite Mediterranean herb. And if you like variegated foliage, you no longer need to turn to ornamentals, for even basil comes in colors—'Pesto Perpetuo' Greek columnar basil has green-and-white leaves as lovely as, and far tastier than, the newest variegated heuchera. Also new to Rose Marie's catalog is "chicken scratch" seed mix, which offers one green or another in bloom most of the year to keep your chickens eating enough greens so that their eggs contain healthy omega-3 fatty acids.

ROSE MARIE'S PICKS

While her firm recommendation is always to grow what you most like to eat, here is a short list of edibles Rose Marie particularly recommends:

'Seascape' strawberries, which are day neutral, with big berries and a sweet, delicious flavor.

'Legend' tomatoes, which are big, delicious red tomatoes that mature early and keep on producing. Her favorite slicing tomatoes are 'Glory' and 'Cherokee Purple'. "Don't even bother with 'Brandywine' or one of those shy producers," she advises. For cherry tomatoes, Rose Marie grows the flashy 'Sun Gold' and 'Red Pearl'.

Heirloom broccoli raab, a nutritious vegetable more like turnip greens than broccoli, with a slightly bitter flavor in its small bud heads and leaves. Simply sauté the leaves and heads in olive oil with a little hot pepper and chopped garlic.

'Australian Yellow' lettuce, an especially gorgeous lettuce with big chartreuse leaves that taste sweet and look as pretty in the salad bowl as trimming pots and flower beds.

Leaf lettuces, such as the Nichols Garden blend of ten different lettuces called 'Lettuce Alone'. Such mixes don't form heads so can be harvested when quite young and then left to grow again. Each time you cut, leave at least a two-inch stub so that the growing tip remains, and they'll quickly sprout again. Plant, snip, repeat.

Arugula, which comes easily from seed, gives a big flavor punch in a small space, and is pretty even when it bolts and flowers. Because arugula grows so aggressively, you should grow it by itself away from the rest of the lettuces.

Jimmy Nardello's sweet frying pepper, which hails from southern Italy, is bred for frying in olive oil, and has been grown for more than a hundred years in the United States because of its spicy yet sweet taste.

Leeks, which are expensive to buy and easy to grow, two good criteria for growing your own at home.

Edible pea pods, because you can grow several plants in a fairly small footprint and because high-quality frozen pea pods are not readily available. 'Cascadia' and 'Sugar Sprint' are delicious, productive, and easy to grow on a tripod tied together from three-foot lengths of bamboo.

Edible pea pods consort with bronze fennel in a pleasing contrast of fresh green and feathery textures and colors.

Edible Flowers

Flowers you can eat may be the ultimate ornamental edibles. Many kinds are delicious, livening up the plate as well as your taste buds. But remember to do your homework because some flowers, like those of monkshood and foxglove, are deadly poisonous. No worry with the flowers listed here, all of which are easy to grow, pretty in the garden, and perfectly safe to eat:

- Pansies are available much of the year and can be tossed into salads or used to garnish cake or cookies. The smaller violas and Johnny-jump-ups are particularly charming. You can use pansies to trim beds and pots, or mix them in with peas or other vegetable plantings.
- Chive blossoms add visual spark to salads as well as a spicy taste.
- Rose petal jam was made by the Greeks; today we stir rose petals into fruit

punch, float a few silky blossoms in ice tea, or garnish a sandwich with these iconic petals.

● Calendula are bright and cheerful flowers that grow easily from seed, and while they don't have much of a taste, they do liven up the looks of a casserole or salad.

● Borage blossoms are such an intricate shape and lovely blue color that I grow

Borage blossoms add beauty to soups, salads, and dinner plates, and taste like cucumber.

them just to pick and toss into salads and soups or use as garnishes.

- Old-fashioned nasturtiums are perhaps the most familiar and easiest to grow edible flower, and one of my very favorite of all flowers.

Nasturtium leaves and flowers are tasty and colorful additions to salads and sandwiches, especially the 'Alaska' series with variegated leaves.

Why do gardeners look down their noses at nasturtiums? If we could forget their slightly common reputation and see these powerhouses of summer color with fresh eyes for a moment, we might all become rabid nasturtium fanciers. Which is a state I've wallowed in for some time, poking nasturtium seeds in every bit of soil I can find.

Consider that nasturtiums are the easiest of summer annuals, growing quickly from seed. They're long blooming and drought tolerant, and they come in trailing, climbing, and bushy forms. Leaves and flowers are edible, with a peppery, watercress-like taste that perks up a salad. So why do I so rarely see nasturtiums growing in gardens besides my own?

Perhaps it's because we all remember carting soggy Dixie cups full of soil and a couple of nasturtium seeds home from grade school. When the poor vines sprouted on the windowsill, no doubt light deprived and prodded along by little fingers, they always looked bedraggled. But bloom they did, just as the ones I plant each year beneath a hedge of bamboo flower their heads off in that most difficult of situations. Just because nasturtiums grow so readily from seed that every kid has a go at it doesn't mean they aren't perfectly desirable plants.

Because of the old-fashioned charm of their sweet-faced flowers, nasturtiums are all too often relegated to the cottage garden. But these are surprisingly versatile flowers, managing to look right at home wherever they're planted. The famed artist-gardener Gertrude Jekyll employed nasturtiums in her carefully orchestrated herbaceous borders. In midsummer she planted nasturtium seeds to grow up and fill in when mounds of perennial baby's breath (*Gypsophila paniculata*) died down. The great flower gardener Christopher Lloyd sequenced his borders with a different type of nasturtium. "There's no more rewarding nasturtium than this," wrote Lloyd of the perennial climbing *Tropaeolum tuberosum*. He grew these vines in the Long Border at his famous garden, Great Dixter, draped over the other plants so that as flowers faded in late summer, the colorful, spurred little nasturtium blooms could take over and carry the show.

Seed companies and nurseries offer a wide variety of nasturtiums. 'Jewel' and fragrant 'Gleam' are both desirable kinds that hold their flowers well up above the lily-pad-shaped leaves. The new 'Tom Thumb Black Velvet' is dramatically dark red, as is the appropriately named 'Mahogany'. Then there's 'Empress' with its blue-green leaves and scarlet flowers.

Botanically, nasturtiums belong to the genus *Tropaeolum*. The old-fashioned kind we see most often, and no doubt grew in our long-ago Dixie cups, are *T. majus*. No wonder nasturtiums prefer bright sunlight, for they hail from South America. These rugged flowers do just fine in lean soil and drought, and in fact prefer such arid conditions.

You can eat every bit of nasturtium plants, and people have grown them for centuries for their edibility as well as their near-neon color. The blossoms not only spark up a salad but can also be used in stir-fries. Fillings can be wrapped in their spicy-tasting leaves. The unripe seedpods are pickled and used as a caperlike condiment and garnish.

Nasturtiums are grown in vegetable gardens not only to brighten up the scene but also because they repel pests and attract beneficial insects. They also trap or "collect" aphids, which is both a virtue and a drawback. If aphids are hanging out on your nasturtiums, they aren't plaguing other plants. However, it may mean you need to blast your nasturtiums regularly with a hard jet of water to rid them of all those pesky aphids.

The common name *nasturtium* means "nose-twister" or "nose-tweaker" because of their tangy, peppery taste and smell. If you give them half a chance, these familiar little beauties will turn your head as well as your nose. Nothing could be easier and more rewarding to grow, nor as useful in the garden, vase, or salad bowl.

A former food writer, restaurant reviewer, and cooking teacher, Joan loves stepping out her front door to clip a few herbs to toss into whatever dish she's concocting for friends and family. Her metal herb spiral holds plants up in the air, close at hand and easy to snip.

VEGGIE VISUALS KICKED UP A NOTCH: JOAN CAINE'S EDIBLE SPIRAL

Art intersects gardening in Joan Caine's edible garden, which is as easy to care for as it is beautiful. She's kicked vegetable visuals up a notch with raised beds made of recycled metal, shaped as sinuously as a Richard Serra sculpture. Dominating the front garden, the shiplike swirl of metal, sprouting bursts of herbs and veggies, is located right outside the front door on the former front lawn.

"Friends see my garden and ask how I do it, because I have my own business and work all the time," says Joan, a management consultant and avid foodie. "I tell them it's tremendously easy to care for. I have great affection for my garden."

As a former cooking instructor, food writer, and restaurant reviewer, Joan has been growing vegetables ever since college, when she lived in Washington, DC. She fondly tells the story of her first plot in a community garden, which was luckily right next to the plot worked by a retired chef, who taught her all about organics. Joan has put the lessons to use in her new garden, where plants grow healthy and pest free in compost-rich soil elevated in open-bottomed, two-foot-high steel planting beds for perfect drainage.

Joan Caine, an enthusiastic cook and vegetable gardener, tore up the grass in her front garden to make room for a sculptural take on raised beds. Cameron Scott designed the recycled Cor-Ten steel beds that swoop around the central wedding-cake-of-a-bed that holds herbs piled upon herbs.

Caine told designer Cameron Scott she wanted a garden crafted of sustainable materials in which to grow herbs, lettuces, and vegetables to use in her daily cooking. Cameron came up with a solution so sculptural that the front garden looks great even in the dead of winter. He used Cor-Ten, or weathering/architectural

How often have you seen a structure so stunningly original yet dirt-gardening practical? Chives, radicchio, lettuces, carrots, mint, kale, and lovage are just a few of the herbs and vegetables Joan cultivates right outside her front door in raised beds as handsome as they are easy to care for.

steel, which starts out black when it's raw and then turns a rich rust color but never rusts through. He coated the inside of the beds with a natural rubber product to protect the metal from leaching into the soil. The steel is so thin it doesn't take up much space, and it heats the soil up in springtime, getting Joan's vegetables off to a good start. "Her vegetables have just jumped right out of the beds," says Cameron. "The tomatoes love the extra heat." The recycled steel poles Cameron used to anchor the beds serve double duty as trellising as well as support for the beds themselves.

The pièce de résistance is the smaller bed in the center, which spirals around like a snail's shell, curling four feet high and filled with herbs. Condolike in its utilization of space, this herbal centerpiece sprouts oregano, lovage, thyme, sorrel, coriander, marjoram, chives, and more chives in a footprint not much bigger than a hatbox. "I probably shouldn't have planted mint," says Joan ruefully, pointing out the happily spreading fragrant leaves. "I do love it, though," she adds brightly. "I just keep ripping it out."

The process of turning a typical blank-slate front lawn into a productive piece of art included ripping out grass, laying a bed of gravel, nestling the metal sheets down into the gravel a few inches, then adding a top layer of crushed granite. The outer-ring planting bed is two feet high, ideal for tending without stooping; the inner spiral rises two feet higher to great effect. The metal started out black, rusting to a weathered-looking orange-brown patina. Cameron filled the beds with a rich mix of soil and compost, which Joan refreshes twice a year with more compost and nutrients.

Other than that, she waters by hand, plants, and harvests, experimenting with new varieties every spring. "I start and end my day out here, checking in with my plants, talking to them," says Joan. "This garden gives me so much joy."

Planting for Style and Taste

In easy-to-care-for, small-space gardening, every plant needs to earn its square foot of soil as well as reliably produce. Ornamentals need to shine in more than one season; edibles need to look pretty as well as taste good.

Plant edibles as ornamentally as you do your flowers, and you make the most of their appearance. Chives make a vigorous, spiky little hedge topped with little balls of lavender flowers, golden oregano is as pretty a front-of-the-border plant as you'll find anywhere, and blueberries are handsome plants with striking fall color. Purple or tricolored sage and rosemary are every bit as useful in the border as clipped, chopped, and stirred into soups and stews.

It was an ornate urn planted up with a bunch of rainbow chard that first alerted me to the ornamental possibilities of edibles. Placed where the sun glowed through the chard's luminous, multicolored stems, the pot was a startlingly gorgeous centerpiece of a formal garden. And it was a bunch of chard! Or how about the dramatic structure lent by fat splays of rhubarb leaves, or gardens hedged in evergreen blueberries (*Vaccinium* 'Sunshine Blue')?

Elegant edible gardening is as much about style of planting as it is about the beauty of the individual plant. You can choose the most gorgeous of vegetables and make little of their looks by planting them in rows in the middle of an arid field. It's a matter of organizing your edibles as ornamentally as you do shrubs, annuals, and perennials.

Skirt a purple artichoke with a ruff of silvery artemisia or mix some ruby-stemmed, fat-leafed rhubarb into a garden bed, and you're creating combinations as artful as any in the most ornamental of borders. Of course, it doesn't hurt to start with the best-looking vegetables and cultivars.

Garden architect David Pfeiffer in his kitchen garden with his wirehaired fox terrier, Stella (foreground), and Irish terrier, Dexter.

EDIBLES AS ORNAMENTALS: DAVID PFEIFFER'S INSPIRED KITCHEN GARDEN

From circular raised beds made of galvanized steel culverts to the ground cover of champagne-scented strawberries, David Pfeiffer's garden looks as good as it tastes. "This isn't a production food garden," says David as he strolls the herb-lined paths, picking a musk strawberry here, a leaf of lemon verbena there.

You won't find straight, tidy rows, an orchard, or a vegetable patch in this neo–Garden of Eden. Instead, chives grow beneath peach trees, golden oregano covers the ground, and the dining arbor drips with purple grapes and fuzzy kiwis. After dinner, guests need merely to reach up to pick dessert.

David is a landscape architect who believes the moniker "garden architect" better captures what he does with the intimate, plant-rich gardens he designs.

Nowhere is this more evident than in his own garden on Vashon Island, southwest of Seattle. His water-view acreage gradually segues from highly ornamental garden rooms around the house, to loose groupings of perennials and grasses, to meadows crisscrossed with mown paths. The surprise is that the kitchen garden

Beneath the arbor is shady repose; the view out is toward the sun-drenched pond and kitchen garden.

Strawberries burgeon around the base of bottomless raised beds made from sheets of galvanized metal. The raised beds hold fruit trees and cut-and-come-again lettuces at just the right height for picking and snipping.

just outside the dining room is as highly designed and dazzling as the rest of this sumptuous garden.

In David's garden, the visuals are as important as flavor. Every plant, from leeks to lettuces, is mined for its ornamental qualities. You enter the kitchen garden by strolling through raised beds of fruit trees and herbs. A hedge of currants along the driveway mingles with orange daylilies and purple-flowering hardy geraniums. Lemon thyme surrounds the pond that centers the cozy graveled seating terrace. Rhubarb's glossy red stems and fat leaves are shown off by an interplanting of fluffy yellow Japanese forest grass (*Hakonechloa macra* 'All Gold'). "I can't bring myself to eat the leeks," he admits. "They're such a great architectural element in the border."

Circular raised beds are a practical as well as an architectural feature of the kitchen garden. David shaped sheets of galvanized metal intended for drainage culverts into circles forty inches tall, left open on the bottom for good drainage. The metal heats up the soil in the spring, encouraging tomatoes and vegetables to ripen more quickly. Each raised bed is centered with a different kind of fruit tree: cherry, frost peach, Asian pear. Arugula and a variety of leafy Italian lettuces foam up around the tree trunks. Their colors, ranging from lime green to dark purple, in textures from ruffled to oak leaf, create a pretty tapestry beneath the trees. All are cut-and-come-again lettuces that can be clipped for salads four or five times before needing to be replanted. Many of the raised beds are festooned with bright orange and yellow nasturtiums, edible blooms David picks to garnish green salads. "My tastes have changed so much," says David. " Now when clients ask for pots, I think about herbs, food and texture, not flowers."

Isn't such an intensely planted garden a lot of work? David says not. "Once I get through spring weeding, which can be intense, it only takes me two hours a week to groom the garden." David's realistic approach adds to the efficiency. "I encourage what's doing well and get rid of the rest," he explains. "I try to minimize the size of the planting area while maximizing the impact." He allows ground covers to spread and smother weeds, and self-seeders like nasturtiums populate the garden.

His low-maintenance manifesto? "I watch what's happening naturally and enhance it, rather than fight it."

David Pfeiffer's garden is an inspired mix of formal and informal, ornamental and edible, as in this jagged silvery artichoke juxtaposed against the repetition of clipped boxwoods in stone pots.

The kitchen garden is let loose to grow billowy and lush within the crisp lines of clipped little boxwood hedges and circular metal raised beds.

The outdoor dining room not only is comfortably shaded but also affords guests a chance to reach up and pick green 'Interlaken' or blue-black 'Glenora' grapes for dessert.

Useless Bay Coffee Company's landscape is an impressionistic haze of edibles. While the herbs, vegetables, lettuces, and fruit need some tinkering through the seasons to look their best, the landscape offers up low-maintenance lessons like plant thickly, consider combinations, and let plants live out their full life cycle. But most of all, this fascinating and beautiful garden illustrates that when edibles are planted and cared for so ornamentally, there's no need for any other kinds of plants, except maybe a tree or two.

THE EDIBLE-IZING OF LANGLEY: A CUT-AND-EAT STREETSIDE GARDEN

Can an edible landscape revitalize a small-town street? Proprietor Des Rock has rocked the Whidbey Island, Washington, town of Langley with the garden around his coffee shop on 2nd Street. The rich scent of roasting coffee wafting from the little metal building may draw people in, but it's the rare pleasure of snacking on berries and relaxing in the scent of sun-warmed herbs every bit as much as the delicious coffee that has made Useless Bay Coffee Company the hub of island life.

It's hard to run an errand without catching the scent of lemon balm or lavender from the cottage-garden-like burst of plants that spills over a split-rail fence. There's nothing shy about the "look-at-me" dynamism of the plants that lap against the sidewalk and burgeon over fences, along pathways, and beside patios.

This edible garden is truly a gift to the street, for it burgeons out to meet the sidewalk with luscious, tasty, fragrant plants just asking passersby to pause, sniff, pick a berry or two.

Passersby on their way to the neighboring post office and library slow down to admire the red Shirley poppies, carpet of lavender-blooming thyme, dill maze, and towering corn and sunflowers. When you see the exuberance of this little garden you realize how rarely we see commercial landscapes with such character. City Hall, across the street, has been inspired to plant their own little edible landscape in raised beds, lining 2nd Street with lettuces, apples, and chard.

What's low-maintenance and easy-care about such a dynamic landscape? First and foremost, the edibles do double duty as ornamentals. Who needs the shrubs and perennials when vegetables and fruit look so fetching? Planted so ornamentally, a productive garden is all you need for eating and appearance's sake. Part of this is the loose, artistic way in which the edibles are used in the landscape. No rows of vegetables here. Ground covers like golden oregano fill in to keep down weeds, lettuces trim the beds, and chives are planted in a little hedge. All this makes maintenance easier, for there's no weeding between rows, and plants gone to seed or past their prime appear a beautiful part of the overall composition.

Passersby stop to wonder over froths of asparagus gone to seed or marvel over the plump lettuces lining the sidewalk. A young cook steps out from the kitchen to snip some chives or basil to flavor a panini sandwich. The coffee shop's landscape

A feathery veil of asparagus gone to seed drapes over self-seeded feverfew and poppies.

Owner Des Rock plans an entire field of artichokes out behind the coffee shop; artichokes are a fixture of the garden for their silvery gray architectural foliage.

is as popular with flocks of tiny, twittering birds as it is with children. The wrens and chickadees rustle through the berry bushes, cling to the top of the sunflowers, and scratch around through the herbs. Parents dare not pass by Useless Bay Coffee Company if they're in a hurry, for their children are liable to plop right down in the garden to sniff and snack.

To sip coffee outdoors is to be enveloped in the life of the garden. It's the constant, seasonal change of fruit and vegetables that draws people in to linger, touch, eat, and relax surrounded by growing food in this most public of landscapes. Proprietor Des hopes customers will taste the red currants that remind him of his English childhood, pinch a sprig of rosemary, snack on the blueberries. "I encourage people to pick things," he says, then grins, "I took all the rhubarb home myself."

After making the unconventional decision to feature food outside as well as inside his shop, Des's next move was to hire glass artist and gardener Elaine Michaelides, who plants and cares for the garden like the evolving work of art that it is. She emphasizes the garden's dynamism and seasonal change, which is one of its biggest attractions. Pea vines flowering mean spring has arrived in Langley; when the sunflowers grow so large they droop their seed-rich heads, autumn must be lurking around the corner.

A stand of mint is left to flower against the rockery. Lettuces, arugula, fava beans, raspberries, and artichokes are allowed to grow, spread, and mature. If not clipped for the kitchen or snacked on by customers, the plants are left to go to seed, to lapse into beautiful senescence, to the delight of both birds and people. Feverfew, poppies, nasturtiums, and alliums are encouraged to fill in between the fruits and vegetables.

Those passing by are constantly asking what this or that plant is, wondering how to cook with it, how to grow it themselves. Elaine shares plants with the community as generously as Des shares coffee grounds for compost—people are encouraged to bring a pail and dig into the fragrant pile of grounds stored away on the side of the shop. The community has responded in kind, sharing their herbs, vegetables, and flowers from neighboring gardens.

Elaine grows many of the plants from seed, including a dill spiral and a flock of furry clary sages that look more fauna than flora. Fava beans grow along the fence, where their black-and-white blossoms attract attention. People stop in their tracks to exclaim over the gigantic silvery cardoons. "Des lets me play out here; he encourages me to keep going with it," Elaine says. She's always wanted to create an ornamental landscape that can be eaten, and she loves how everyone, especially young people, asks about the plants.

"The garden isn't a fringe thing or an adornment," says Des. "It's key to what we're doing here." He picks parsley, chives, sage, basil, oregano, and mint to use in herbed aioli; arugula and lettuces are used in salads and panini. The gardens are trimmed in hedges of lavender and chives, or with rows of purple, green, and speckled lettuces.

It's almost a shock to recognize the changeable beauty of berries, vegetables, and herbs on full display growing along the sidewalk. This very public garden is both sensory pleasure and a reminder of the gratification to be had in growing your own food. Des and Elaine plan to further enchant the town by planting a field of artichokes out back. "If it's not a tree, you can eat it," remains the motto of this duo who double-handedly are edible-izing the town of Langley.

The split-rail fence separating parking strip from coffee shop garden is as thickly planted outside as in, with an inspired mix of rosemary, poppies, and feverfew grounded by a hugely splayed and veined rhubarb leaf.

THE PRETTIEST EDIBLES

These are just a few edibles that are as beautiful as they are tasty:

Rainbow chard. With luminous stems in shades of yellow through burgundy, this used-to-be-humble vegetable lights up the cool season garden so brightly that it's worth growing even if you never sautée a leaf.

'Graffiti' cauliflower. 'Graffiti' is as solid purple as a grape, so it shows up beautifully in the garden. However, it loses its intense color when cooked, so add a splash of vinegar to the water to preserve its drama on the plate.

Rhubarb. Grow this ruby-stemmed, statuesque beauty in the flower bed, where its fat, textural splay of low-growing leaves contrasts pleasingly with most ornamentals.

Kale. Kale leaves are thick and crinkly and come in a mix of colors. 'Winter Red' is one of the darkest and showiest.

Meyer lemon tree. In most climates these handsome trees need to winter indoors in a conservatory, sunny window, or heated sun porch, although they're surprisingly hardy, surviving temperatures down into the high teens. It's well worth the trouble of dragging their pots inside, for these little trees are easily kept pruned to a manageable size, have fragrant flowers and shiny leaves, and bear fruit far more flavorful than standard lemons. Improved Meyer lemon trees come on dwarfing rootstock, which grows into a bushy tree four to six feet tall with bright yellow fruit gratifyingly outsized for the tree's tidy size and shape.

Lettuces. Whether you call them salad bowl lettuces, leaf lettuces, or mesclun mixes, a ruffled mix of them makes a lovely edible ground cover or trim for a bed or pot. 'Lollo' has deeply curled leaves; 'Merlot' has pretty grape-colored leaves and holds up well in the garden; and the bright 'Red Sails' has excellent heat resistance, while the leaves have a handsome, distinctive oak shape. The new butter oak lettuce 'Flashy' has light green leaves splashed with red.

Raddichio

Italian purple artichoke. Artichoke 'Violetto' is a compact version of these most dramatic of edibles, with silvery, spiny foliage that persists through the season and in summer is topped with showy maroon artichokes.

Fava beans. With their uniquely checkered black-and-white flowers, favas would be sold as ornamentals if the nutritious beans weren't edible.

Pumpkins. Pumpkin vines can grow ratty as the season progresses, but nothing is more spectacular come autumn than pumpkins ripening in the garden. Kids love ghost pumpkins like the tennis-ball-size white 'Baby Boo', whose pallor in the garden is startling. My favorite remains the old-fashioned French heirloom' Cinderella'. This intensely orange-red-colored fruit is slightly flattened in shape with deep ridges. It grows easily from seed and is good for eating and for carving. Popular in France since the 1800s, this is supposedly the pumpkin that Cinderella's fairy godmother turned into a coach with a wave of her wand.

Beets. 'Bull's Blood' has burgundy stems and leaves; 'Chioggia' has white-and-pink ringed roots as well as dark leaves. If you leave a few beets to go to seed, they grow into dramatic reddish spires with multiple heads.

Garlic scapes and leeks. These add height to the garden with their sinuously curving and looping stems and heads.

Peas. 'Blauschokker Purple Podded' is as ornamental as it is delicious. These pea vines bloom with red and violet flowers in spring, followed by glossy purple pods that can be eaten early like snow peas or left to ripen.

Runner beans. These beans come in dwarf forms for smaller gardens, with flowers in shades from hot red to orange, pink, white, and bicolored. You can mix in sweet peas, grow them up a big sunflower, or grow them on a tripod of sticks to form a shady teepee. 'Sunset' has pink flowers; 'Painted Lady' has flowers that are showy orange and white.

Garlic scapes

Blauschokker Purple Podded' pea

Keep It Simple

Many of the same "Keep it Simple" techniques and skills that apply to ornamental plantings work equally well for edibles.

- Begin by preparing your soil. All edibles do best with good drainage and well-composted soil. Since you don't have the time or energy to waste being anything but a successful gardener, read up on what each herb, fruit, and vegetable needs to thrive before planting (this is a compelling reason to start slowly with edibles, adding just a few new kinds to your garden every spring or fall).

- Use your precious time, space, and sun to grow the plants you most want to eat and cook with, and/or those not readily available at local farmers' markets. Squashes take up a good deal of garden space, and I've never seen a farmers' market without an abundance of inexpensive zucchini in August. Fresh baby lettuces and arugula are expensive and questionably organic, if available, and so easy, quick, and pretty to grow from seed.

- "Right plant, right place": This most important of mantras could have been invented for growing food because fruit and vegetables often have more exacting requirements than ornamentals. Check with your local master gardener/extension service or in books written for your region to find which fruits and vegetables flourish in the temperatures and soils you can offer. It doesn't matter how pretty the leaves on a fig tree if the fruit won't ripen in your climate (figs require at least the temperatures of USDA zone 7). And no matter how potentially delicious the tomato, if it takes seventy days to ripen and you live at higher elevations with a brief growing season, you won't enjoy figuring out what to do with all those green tomatoes come September.

- Follow your taste buds when choosing what to grow; if you really love a certain vegetable or fruit, go ahead and try it. Perhaps you can ripen a 'Brown Turkey' fig if you grow it as an espalier against a south- or west-facing wall, even if you live in a colder zone than it would prefer. I've seen Seattle gardeners ripening eggplant in pots soaking up the sun on a south-facing roof. But if you overdo the accommodating gymnastics, you defeat the goal of simplicity. Remember that there are plenty of herbs and vegetables that will no doubt thrive in conditions you can offer reasonably easily.

- While it's tempting to skimp on infrastructure, don't. Support structures are every bit as important to growing vegetables as they are to propping up our figures as we grow older. Just think of how edibles mature in a few short weeks or months and give them the support they'll need, whether it be cages for tomatoes, trellises

Texture, color, and shape are every bit as important in determining combinations of edibles as of ornamentals. Here a drape of spiny rosemary plays off the rough sides of an urn stuffed with pansies, pale sage, and deep-purple chard.

for beans and peas, or a sturdy arbor to grow grapes. Just figure your plants will need more structure than you'd ever imagine and offer it ahead of when it's needed, to save yourself work and lost food in the long run. Remember there's no way to gracefully retrofit a drooping, wilted, or contorted vine—props not only support but also help the plant to grow beautifully and healthfully.

- Good gardens are made one combination at a time. Edibles don't exist outside this rule, even though they've too often been grown in rows or at least grouped with others of their kind. Pea pods look great piggybacking up a bronze fennel, beans can be grown up sturdy sunflowers as well as a trellis, and low-growing herbs and lettuces are ideal for edging beds, borders, and pots. For a pot as ornamental as it is delicious, center a big container or raised bed with a columnar apple or bay tree, surrounded by geraniums, strawberries, and lettuces, with nasturtiums dangling down the side for a blast of summer color.

- Make every inch of dirt and every hour of effort pay off by choosing double-duty plants. Blueberries are great-looking landscape or hedging plants with the most nutritious of berries, violas and calendulas brighten the garden and vase as well as the salad bowl, and strawberries make a beautiful and tasty ground cover. Artichokes add height and structure to the garden; sage and rosemary are sturdy, handsome shrubs.

- Toss pest- and disease-prone plants. If you've done your best to provide soil, water, and nutrients and a plant still refuses to flourish, compost it and start over in a different location, or not at all. There's never a shortage of great plants beckoning, and no reason to struggle with something ill suited to your location or style of gardening.

- All the same weed-elimination techniques that apply to ornamentals also apply when growing vegetables.

- Don't overgroom, for your mother isn't looking over your shoulder anymore (or if she is, invite her to help weed). Since edibles cycle quickly through the seasons, constant tidying up denudes the garden of great plant theatrics. Relax with the maintenance and let at least some of your arugula and lettuces bolt, asparagus go to seed, dill and chives flower, rainbow chard grow tall and lanky. Birds and insects love the added ripeness of overblown plantings, and you'll learn to appreciate the changing beauty plants offer in all their life stages.

Chard grown long and lanky consorts with sweet pea vines in a surprisingly synchronistic combination that never would have happened if the chard had been pulled out the minute it started to bolt.

Resources

NURSERIES AND CATALOGS Most nurseries carry edibles, and most often the vegetables, fruits, and herbs best suited to where you live and garden. Make friends with knowledgeable nursery staff, ask questions, and take advantage of all the information and plants available at good local nurseries.

For a wider variety, or for unusual species and cultivars, you may need to order plants and seeds by mail. Here's a short list of fine sources around the country, many with catalogs and Web pages that are themselves an education:

Johnny's Selected Seeds, (877) 564-6697, www.johnnyseeds.com. This thriving seed business, established in 1973 in Albion, Maine, offers as complete a selection of seed, much of it organic and heirloom, as you'll find anywhere. It's worth ordering the catalog as a reference tool even if you never place an order—but you will.

John Scheepers Kitchen Garden Seeds, (860) 567-6086, www.kitchengardenseeds.com. From jicama to chervil, gourds to tomatillos, if you can eat it, this Bantam, Connecticut, catalog offers it, with a few flowers and recipes thrown in.

Nichols Garden Nursery, (800) 422-3985, www.nicholsgardennursery.com. This family-owned business in Oregon's Willamette Valley specializes in rare and unusual herbs, vegetables, and flowers. They've been in business since 1949 and have introduced many plants and seeds, including elephant garlic, true tea plants, intriguing salad blends, and ecology lawn mixes, with an emphasis on plants for the gardener-cook.

Raintree Nursery, (888) 770-8358, www.raintreenursery.com. If they can grow it in Morton, Washington, a small logging town in the shadow of Mount Rainier, it'll thrive anywhere. This could be the motto for this nursery's outstandingly varied offerings of fruit trees, berries, and unusual edibles from around the world.

Renee's Garden Seeds, (888) 880-7228, www.reneesgarden.com. Renee Shepherd, operating out of Felton, California, is a leader in the organic grow-your-own movement. She offers thoughtfully selected herb, flower, and vegetable seeds from around the world. Renee is known especially for knowledgeable selectivity, so you won't find everything here, just the best—her fragrant flowers, with a great selection of sweet peas, pretty seed packets, and gourmet vegetables.

Seed Savers Exchange, www.seedsavers.org. Dedicated to promoting garden biodiversity through saving and sharing heirloom seeds, this nonprofit group has distributed a million rare seeds since 1975.

Territorial Seed Company, (800) 626-0866, www.territorialseed.com. Located in Cottage Grove, Oregon, Territorial emphasizes the unusual ('Drunken Woman Frizzy Headed Lettuce' and cylindrical 'Monument Chinese Cabbage') and the especially hardy, and sells plants, including fruit trees and bushes, as well as seed. Long a champion of off-season gardening, they offer an abundance of plants suited to fall, winter, and earliest spring harvests.

BOOKS Every part of the country has its own reliable reference books. Visit your local public library, a good local bookstore, or a local arboretum or public garden library. Browse through the stacks, files, and magazines to find which books appeal to you and ask questions about which references focus on your region. See also these less place-specific books for inspiration:

The Bountiful Container by Rose Marie Nichols McGee and Maggie Stuckey (Workman, 2002) is a best-selling paperback on growing an impressively wide range of edibles in containers, from a duo of hard-working women who know whereof they write.

The Complete Book of Edible Landscaping by Rosalind Creasy (Sierra Club Books, 1982) is the forerunner of Haeg's more current manifesto, and the book that started the beautiful vegetable garden movement. Look for an updated version in January 2010.

Creative Vegetable Gardening, revised edition, by Joy Larkcom (Mitchell Beazley, 2008). Larkcom is the queen of British vegetable gardening, and her newest book pulls together design, cultivation, and a great visual dictionary of edible plants. Her chapter "Potager Management" and the many photos of raised bed possibilities are worth the modest price of this oversize softcover book, which is as colorful as the edible gardens it extols.

Edible Estates: Attack on the Front Lawn, a project by Fritz Haeg with chapters by Diana Balmori, Rosalind Creasy, Fritz Haeg, Michael Pollan, and Lesley Stern (Metropolis Books, 2008). This is the most hip, political book on vegetable gardening you'll ever read. Haeg is a young Los Angeles architect who decries lawn and traditional ornamental gardens as he makes his case for growing vegetables instead in his manifesto of a chapter, "Full-Frontal Gardening."

Fresh Food from Small Spaces by R. J. Ruppenthal (Chelsea Green, 2008). An attorney wrote this intriguing little book, detailing how he's fed his family by gardening indoors, on balconies, and in small urban plots. Do you think, especially if you garden on a condo deck or in a community garden, that you could grow 10 to 20 percent of the food your family needs? Read and be convinced that sprouting, espaliers, containers, and cloches, among other inexpensive techniques and devices, can turn wherever you live into a food factory.

Gardener Cook by Christopher Lloyd (Frances Lincoln Ltd, 1998). While the recipes have a strong British flavor, with a number of puddings, this venerable gardener's intimate connection between what he grows and how he eats is inspiring, as is his emphasis on freshness and simplicity.

The Garden Primer, second edition, by Barbara Damrosch (Workman, 2008) is an updated look at all the basics from a thorough, practical, organic point of view.

Recipes from a Kitchen Garden and *More Recipes from a Kitchen Garden* by Renee Shepherd can be ordered at www. reneesgarden.com. These little books are fun and lively, with easy, everyday recipes and advice on harvesting, storing, and selecting a wide variety of edibles.

Rosalind Creasy's Recipes from the Garden by Rosalind Creasy (Tuttle Press, 2008). Recipes and glamorous color photos from the kitchen garden, with a lively emphasis on Italian techniques.

ONLINE RESOURCES There are a multitude of Web pages and blogs on kitchen gardening and cooking from the garden. Here are a couple worth a look:

Eat The View, www.eattheview.org, is a political campaign to transform lawns into productive vegetable gardens, with high-profile examples and ambition.

Kitchen Gardens International, www.kitchengardeners.org, emphasizes organic growing and home cooking with an international perspective, raising it a cut above many of the more personal Web pages.

A raised planter holds a riot of color so intense it'd warm up the chilliest spring day. Orange tulips need to be planted every year, but with proper drainage as in this planter, the hyacinths and pansies may well be perennial.

Carefree Containers

CONTRARY TO POPULAR WISDOM, plants confined to containers and window boxes are less labor intensive than beds and borders. Pots have earned their labor-intensive rep because gardeners tend toward potting up complicated living bouquets of annuals. Which is one approach, but there are many more simple, elegant ways to design pots, including a limited palette of plants that take to container culture, planting one specimen plant per pot, or even using unplanted pots as sculptural elements in the garden.

Here's the irony—not only are pots featuring a single structural plant, or a couple of well-combined plants, much easier to care for, but they're also more stylish and striking than pots overstuffed with a bunch of different plants.

The beauty of growing your garden in pots is that you control the soil, water, and nutrients, plus it's easy to move the pots about for optimal shade and sun. What plant doesn't look its best raised up and corralled within an encircling edge? Plants that look quite ordinary growing in the ground look quite extraordinary displayed in a pot. Think of a tangled mess of cherry tomatoes emerging from a garden patch versus bright red and yellow tomatoes cascading down the

ABOVE: Who needs color for impact? In an inspired match of plant to pot, the silvery-olive-green grass *Astelia nervosa* 'Westland Red' is a study in dramatic shape and form.

OPPOSITE: The glowing stems of Swiss chard 'Bright Lights' play backdrop to prostrate rosemary, ruffly leaf lettuce 'Revolution', golden sage (*Salvia officinalis* 'Icterina'), and tough little violas that continue to bloom through the worst of winter weather.

This year-round, two-plant composition of Japanese bitter orange (*Poncirus trifoliata* 'Flying Dragon') underplanted with creeping Jenny (*Lysimachia nummularia* 'Aurea') brings drama, color, texture, and structure to the garden. The backdrop of a dark wall makes the most of this simple plant pairing.

sides of a cobalt blue urn. Or a fine-textured specimen like the "bad hair day" contorted wire-netting bush (*Corokia cotoneaster*) that stars in a pot but disappears when planted out in the garden. Whether your entire garden is grown in containers or you use them as accents, pot planting is fun and easy artistry, as well as a practical way to grow flowers, shrubs, and food.

As in any gardening endeavor, you start with the soil. Buy high-quality organic potting soil and refresh it seasonally by topping off with compost and fresh soil. Drainage is essential—make sure your pot has an adequate number of holes in the bottom so that water drains through quickly. Aid drainage and save the surface of your deck or patio by setting the pot up on little feet—one of the best new products around is PotRisers, which are inexpensive, made of recycled material, and best of all so unobtrusive you can't see them beneath the pots even though four of the rubbery little things support a whopping 1600 pounds.

There are only two drawbacks to container gardening, and both are easily remedied. Raised up in pots, plants are more vulnerable to freezing since their roots aren't as well insulated by soil. Use the largest containers you can afford (and are able to move around) in order to give plants the most possible soil around their roots. The second challenge is watering, as plants dry out more quickly in pots than in the ground. Again, the larger the pot the better, for it'll dry out more slowly. You can commit to watering often or install a simple watering device with a liquid reservoir, or a drip system. Many gardeners love to water their pots, as it gives them a chance to check in with their plants, pinch back and tidy, or just meditate with hose in hand.

Containers should be at least twenty-four inches in diameter to give adequate root room. Beyond that, choose pots you love. I've seen displays of totally mismatched pots made harmonious because they reflect a gardener's taste, and I've seen multiples of a single kind of pot used in various sizes and shapes. While the latter looks a little more sophisticated, the former is satisfyingly personal. You can key your pot choice to the style or color of your home's exterior. Or you can set your garden's style with the type of pot you choose; metal, Chinese red, and matte black look contemporary, while urns and box shapes are more traditional. If you aren't sure what to choose, go for pots with a rough, rustic brown finish, which shows off plants beautifully and goes with any architecture or décor.

You can't get much simpler, more elegant, or easier-care than Japanese stones and sedums beneath the branches of wire-netting bush (*Corokia cotoneaster*), a shrub that grows slowly and looks about the same whether or not in leaf and bloom.

A lichen-encrusted trough raises up small specimen plants to be admired close up.

Frost-hardy, evergreen oven's wattle (*Acacia pravissima*) decorates a corner of the garden with its feathery foliage, which looks its best set off in a tall urn.

PLANTS FOR CONTAINER CULTURE

While just about any plant can be grown in a pot, some are far more suited to container culture than others. If you don't want to root-prune and transplant often, choose plants that are naturally petite and slow growing. A useful rule of thumb for harmonious plantings is to limit your colors but go wild with textures.

These plants seem bred for container culture:

- dwarf tomatoes like 'Micro-Tom' and 'Micro-Tina'
- dwarf blueberry 'Top-Hat'
- columnar apple trees
- leaf lettuces
- rainbow chard
- small ornamental grasses like carex, blue fescue, and fountain grass (*Pennisetum alopecuroides* 'Little Bunny')
- dwarf conifers like deodar cedar (*Cedrus deodara* 'Snowsprite') and yew (*Taxus xmedia* 'Hicksii')
- heucheras with their ruffled and colored foliages, especially the showy and long-lasting 'Obsidian', 'Frosted Violet', 'Peach Flambé', and 'Alabama Sunrise'
- hellebores for winter bloom and long-lasting leaves
- bergenia for its fat, paddle-shaped evergreen leaves
- sedums for texture and drought tolerance
- small ferns such as autumn fern (*Dryopteris erythrosora*)
- small shrubs like boxleaf honeysuckle (*Lonicera nitida* 'Lemon Beauty' and 'Baggesen's Gold'), *Hebe* 'Amy' and 'Purpurea', *Nandina domestica* 'Gulf Stream', and *Abelia xgrandiflora* 'Kaleidoscope' and 'Sunrise'
- creeping ground covers to fill in between plants, like golden spike moss, thymes, and *Sedum makinoi* 'Ogon'
- for summer color, coleus, dwarf petunias, geraniums, heliotrope, or your favorite flowers for color and scent

You can mix and match these plants or make an elegant statement by filling a pot with several of the same color heuchera or a single shrub or conifer, or planting a "skim" of sedum across the top of the pot, which emphasizes the texture and shape of the pot and is the easiest care option of all.

Bulbs in Containers

All that bulbs need in order to thrive is sun and good drainage; planting them in pots makes it easy to provide both of these essentials. Raising bulbs up into a pot filled with good soil mix is a surefire way to make sure they don't drown over the winter. And it's easy to move a pot into the sun as bulbs are getting close to bloom time.

Simply layer bulbs in pots in autumn, then enjoy waves of bloom February through June. It's best to use a large pot—one with an interior diameter of at least twenty-four inches is ideal, although I've used smaller pots and still had a fine springtime show.

Tulips, with their long stems and diva looks, grandly fill a pot all by themselves. And since most tulips aren't perennial, it makes sense to grow your tulips in pots, right by the front or back door so you can enjoy them most. Then pull and toss after they fade in spring, and you can use the same pot for summer flowers.

Assembling what you need for mixed winter pots is like gathering the ingredients to bake a cake, except less exacting. What you need is a woody plant for height and structure, low-growing plants to group around its trunk, and several different kinds of bulbs to layer in the soil.

Start with the woody plant—most small trees and shrubs can stay in a pot for several years before being put into the ground. I kept a corkscrew hazel (*Corylus avellana* 'Contorta') in a pot for years before I let it loose to grow happily in the border. Dwarf hinoki cypress are evergreen and slow growing, dogwoods and Japanese maples have a lovely line in winter and decorative foliage in summer. I have a yellow-variegated false holly (*Osmanthus heterophyllus* 'Goshiki') in a pot on the front porch that I string with Christmas lights in December and surround with bacopa in summer; in springtime purple crocus bloom around its trunk. This is easy gardening.

A rustic pot holds a year-round medley of the soft grass *Anemanthele lessoniana* and heucheras 'Plum Pudding', 'Amethyst Mist', and 'Amber Waves', with a coleus and begonia added for summer color.

A bronze-toned sedge serves as backdrop for the willowy stems and delicate drooping bells of *Allium bulgaricum* (a.k.a. *Nectaroscordum siculum* subsp. *bulgaricum*).

Place the tree or shrub in the pot first, with plenty of fresh, well-draining potting soil beneath it. Then put the latest-blooming spring bulbs on the bottom layer, about halfway down inside the pot. These could be late tulips, like the ruffled pink 'Angelique' or deeper pink 'May Wonder', or the darkly elegant 'Queen of the Night'. Use at least seven or nine bulbs—as many as you can squeeze in without touching each other or the sides of the pot (they need plenty of soil for insulation from the cold). Fill in around them, sprinkling in a little bulb food, and cover with a few inches of soil. Then nestle in a layer of midseason bulbs, perhaps hyacinths for fragrance (these are fat bulbs, so you won't be able to use many) or narcissus. Fill in with soil again and add a top layer of early-blooming crocus, grape hyacinth, or little *Iris reticulata*. Water in, patting down the soil until it settles between all the layers of bulbs. At this point you should still have about six inches left at the top of the pot, which you can stuff with ground covers, little ornamental grasses, winter pansies, or perennials. I often use the dark-leafed heucheras, which keep their foliage all winter, a few colorful pansies, and one of the small sedges, like bronze New Zealand hair sedge (*Carex comans*), to droop down the side of the pot.

It's best to keep the pot in a protected spot over the winter, moving it to a sunnier spot in early spring. The warmth will encourage the bulbs to push through the soil and bloom, one kind after another, for a springtime of color.

The bright boxleaf honeysuckle *Lonicera nitida* 'Baggesen's Gold' joins the textural little conifer *Juniperus communis* 'Compressa' as the anchors of a pot stuffed with verbena and cosmos for summer.

Scrumptious Pots

How often do containers appeal to the taste buds as well as the eyes? How many pots have you seen that burst with vitamins as well as leaves and flowers? The edible-filled containers Barbara Libner created for Ravenna Gardens in Seattle look every bit as scrumptious as they taste.

Libner plants greens, herbs, and edible flowers in combinations so colorful and textural they blur the line between ornamental and edible. These are simply gorgeous containers that just happen to hold tasty organic food.

What better way to liven up an outdoor dining area, or any deck, patio, or window box? All these edible pots are planted in early fall to provide greens and herbs well into winter, but the concepts, plants, and ideas would work as well for spring or summer containers, where you'd have a wider range of annuals to mix in with the herbs and greens.

Pansy 'Majestic Giants II Fire' (who names these plants, anyway?) holds court among crisp lettuces 'Mascara' and 'Revolution' and French curly endive in a salad bowl of a pot.

When planted in a glossy rectangular pot, vegetables can hold their own in a formal setting. Here radicchio 'Chioggia Red Preco No. 1', which comes on early and doesn't bolt, anchors one corner of the container. Tricolor sage adds a darker note played against viola 'Skyline Copperfield', variegated thyme, and a burst of taller chives and rosemary for a pot you can graze on for months.

TIPS FOR EDIBLE CONTAINERS

Here are Barbara Libner's tips for edible containers that look as good as they taste:

- **Design.** Libner considers the color, form, and texture of edible plants as if they were ornamentals—which, of course, they are. She crams her pots full to make instant gardens ready to begin harvesting in a few weeks. "Use the veggies as your main design elements," advises Libner. "Their leaves are downright gorgeous."

- **Soil mix.** Use a mix with moisture-retentive capabilities, such as Gardener & Bloome, or any good-quality concoction with plenty of compost mixed in. Libner favors the Cedar Grove brand, made in the Northwest from recycled garden waste. Check out which potting mixes are produced where you live, for they're freshest and haven't been shipped thousands of miles.

- **Pot size.** For tomatoes, use a container that's at least eighteen inches in circumference. Radishes do well in a shallow, wide pot, as do lettuces and most herbs. Libner is planning to add large galvanized troughs to her own garden to grow root vegetables. "I can even see planting potatoes in a nice, deep galvanized trash can, drilled with holes, then just upturning it to harvest," she says.

- **Pick of the plants.** Ornamental cabbage and kale thrive in pots and add great texture and color. Leaf lettuces grow bountifully in confined spaces, are full of nutrients, and are beautifully varied in colors and shapes. Herbs like sage, lemon verbena, chives, basil, and thyme adapt easily to pot culture and are especially useful grown near the kitchen door, kept right at hand so the cook remembers to snip them regularly.

Lavender and white viola 'Sorbet Yesterday, Today and Tomorrow' spark this low, fat pot stuffed with rosemary, variegated thyme (*Thymus vulgaris* 'Silver Posy'), and spinach.

A Gallery of Carefree Containers

Blue-green splays of honey bush (*Melianthus major*) fluff out a rustic urn centered with *Pennisetum glaucum* 'Purple Majesty'.

A birdbath makes a fine pot-on-a-pedestal, planted with a combination of easy-care sedums and hens and chicks (*Sempervivum*). It's a focal point that never needs water (it's undrilled) or fertilizing.

The small pot in front holding primroses is changed out to suit the season, but the sedum-filled and water-filled pots, with the coppery spring foliage of *Spirea japonica* 'Magic Carpet' in the background, anchor this corner of the patio year-round.

A dramatic foliage composition with year-round presence—*Fatsia japonica* grows happily in a pot surrounded by a bed of *Viburnum opulus* 'Nana'.

A drought-tolerant medley of succulents; the dark note is *Aeonium arboreum* 'Zwartkop', with height from *Sedum* 'Autumn Joy' and the icy blue finger (*Senecio mandraliscae*). String of beads (*Senecio rowleyanus*) dangles down the side of the metal container.

The wavy, tall, glossy pot is the star in this green-on-purple composition of hardy bergenia, heuchera, ajuga, and the dwarf striped ornamental grass *Miscanthus sinensis* 'Gold Bar'. Such textural foliage combinations are long lasting and easy care.

A dark, glossy urn holds a selection of durable plants with contrasting shapes and textures, including evergreen *Hebe* 'Clear Skies', golden *Choisya ternata* 'Sundance', and tiny yellow *Sedum makinoi* 'Ogon' for year-round presence. A pale flowering *Abutilon* ×*hybridum* 'Bella Mix', succulent *Echeveria* 'Silver Onion', and the blue flower spikes of *Salvia farinacea* 'Rhea' fill out the composition for summer.

Not many plants could stand up to the harsh conditions on this hot, windy, high-in-the-sky terrace. Succulents like *Aeonium canariense* (in the dark pot at the back), blue-toned *Senecio mandraliscae*, and pig's ear (*Cotyledon orbiculata*), accented by the dark spiky blades of *Phormium* 'Dusky Chief', are up to the job.

Who would have thought just two plants could carry a container through the seasons? A lacy Japanese maple stars in summer, underplanted with *Heuchera* 'Caramel' to fill out the pot year-round.

This summery-looking pot is filled with tough, long-lasting plants like the tall evergreen mountain pepper (*Drimys lanceolata*), *Sedum* 'Button', and the grass *Acorus gramineus* 'Variegata'. A frilly coleus and *Celosia* 'Ice Cream Peach' lend seasonal color.

While this pot is dramatic in its play of light and dark foliages, it's anchored year-round by a sturdy dwarf conifer (*Cryptomeria japonica* 'Black Dragon'), and the only annual that would need springtime replanting is the coleus. The golden creeping Jenny (*Lysimachia nummularia* 'Aurea'), carpet bugle (*Ajuga reptans* 'Black Scallop') with its crinkled leaves, and the weeping brown sedge (*Carex flagellifera*) are all durable through the seasons.

ABOVE: A cluster of watery pots each feature a single type of plant, which draws attention to what is so special about each. Horsetails grow in the tall metal pot, cannas to the left, and carnivorous pitcher plants flank the pot of horsetails. BELOW: Galvanized metal troughs, available at feed stores, are the least expensive large container possible. All you do is punch plenty of holes in the bottom, roll them into place, fill with good soil, and plant. These circular troughs are four feet in diameter, large enough to grow trees and shrubs as well as fruit and vegetables.

Growing tender succulents in smallish pots makes them easy to bring indoors for the winter. Clustering the pots together makes for great design, for the plants' colors, textures, and shapes play off each other. *Echeveria agavoides* 'Red Edge' is in the low pots in the back, *Agave* 'Blue Glow' is in the foreground on the right, and *Agave parryi* 'Cream Spike' is the small, creamy-leafed succulent in the front most pot on the left.

This egg-shaped orange pot holds a sufficient volume of soil that the spirea, euphorbia, and sumac need watering only once a week, even in summer.

Keep It Simple

- Size matters—the bigger the pot, the longer the plants can stay put and the less often you have to water and fertilize. Buy the biggest pots you can afford in order to cut down on maintenance.

- Sometimes the most elegant container of all is left unplanted to stand as a silhouette in the garden. An unplanted container takes on the allure of sculpture, and you notice its texture, color, and shape much more than if plants were gushing out the top or pouring down its sides. And empty containers are much more portable than planted ones, perfect to use as movable focal points, architectural elements, or to fill in where needed through the seasons.

- Not every container needs to look like a bouquet; sometimes fewer plants are better. Remember that "three kinds of plants to a pot" is only a suggestion, not a rule. The height and edge provided by a container show off a single specimen shrub or tree, masses of the same sedum, or even two plants that play off each other's colors or textures. Singling out plants for such attention really makes you see and appreciate them. Often such simple arrangements are more sophisticated than a jumble of plants, let alone being a breeze to care for.

- Don't overlook carpeting ground covers, like low-profile sedums, mosses, and mondo grass, as stand-alone container plants. A little sweep of ground cover adds a textural lid to the composition without detracting from the shape and finish of the container.

- Plants contained are plants dependent, for they get every bit of nutrition from the soil you give them. So make sure it's a nice, rich mix with plenty of compost. Some gardeners mix in a time-release fertilizer at planting time, others dose their containers regularly with a diluted mixture of liquid food, and many do both.

- Water, water, water your pots. Even a rainstorm won't thoroughly soak plants in a pot, and pots beneath the eaves or out in the bright sun need regular watering. On long, hot summer days it's hard to overwater a container.

- For a long-lasting, rewarding container composition, rely on foliage textures, shapes, and colors. The most sophisticated-looking, easy-care pots use a narrow color palette, with the drama coming from contrasting textures.

This voluminous urn lends a year-round sculptural presence; in springtime its glossy, dark bulk plays off silvery senecio and the ephemeral glow of pale narcissus.

Raised up in this tall, simple pot, a durable, drought-tolerant burro's tail sedum (*S. morganianum*) becomes a star.

Proof that color coordination pays off as handsomely with edibles as ornamentals, this Chinese-red pot holds a Monet-like palette of 'Merlot' lettuce, 'Button' sedum, and 'Skyline Copperfield' pansies.

Resources

BOOKS   There are many books on container gardening, but most take an elaborate approach rather than a simplified one. Many of the resources in "Design with Maintenance in Mind" include container gardening. Here are a trio of books to get you started:

The Bountiful Container by Rose Marie Nichols McGee and Maggie Stuckey (Workman, 2002). If you've ever wondered if you can grow corn and eggplant in containers, you'll find a resounding yes as well as practical advice on how to grow these and many more in this bible of edible container gardening.

Pots in the Garden: Expert Design and Planting Techniques by Ray Rogers, with photographs by Richard Hartlage (Timber Press, 2007). This visual guide to container gardening inspires and excites. While many of the pots hold tropicals or masses of annuals, there are plenty of great ideas for simpler compositions of sedum, unplanted pots, or containers showing off a single specimen tree or shrub.

Window Boxes Indoors and Out: 100 Projects and Planting Ideas for All Four Seasons by James Cramer and Dean Johnson (Storey, 1999). The design ideas and inspired plant choices in this stylish and beautifully photographed book work not just for window boxes but for any contained situation, from water troughs to miniature vegetable patches.

ONLINE RESOURCES   **PotLifter**, www.potlifter.com. Soil-and-plant-filled pots are shockingly heavy. How often have you risked the health of your back to move a pot just a foot or two? The PotLifter is an inexpensive, ingenious strap with a lifetime guarantee that enables two people to safely move heavy, awkward pots, root balls, rocks, or sacks of soil.

PotRisers, www.potrisers.com. If you can't find these sturdy little pot feet in your local nurseries, order them here. These clever products, which are invisible under pots, protect decks, help pots drain better, and are ideal for those of us who prefer to feature our plants and pots rather than decorative feet.

'Moonfire' Japanese maple frames a garden scene, its crimson foliage contrasting with both darker and lighter plants. Simple pot plantings and hardscape cuts down on maintenance.

Smart Choices:
Editing Your Plant Picks

RAY BRADBURY SAID, "THE ART LIES IN THE EDIT." He was talking about writing, but it applies every bit as much to gardens.

When I told gardening friends around the country about the topic of this book, I heard a common refrain that ran something like this: "I used to collect plants, and I still love them. But my garden became a nightmare—it wore me out—I just didn't have time—I overdid it." Then came the part about how they had modified their garden, simplified it, or sold it and started over. Those who had gone on to loving their gardens again concluded with something like "Now it's all about choosing fewer, great plants and using them well."

Most of us are lured into garden making by our love of plants. We fall for the juiciness of their life force, how they ebb and flow through the seasons, how they bud, flower, fruit, die down, grow back. The only constant is glorious, voluptuous, fascinating change. We love the sensuality of plants' textures, colors, blooms, and fragrance.

We get hooked on the reciprocity of plants, how they respond to our care. We feel as if we're touching nature, crossing species lines out there in our gardens. We

ABOVE: Long-blooming *Astrantia major* 'Hadspen Blood' is a workhorse of a perennial with spiky little flowers that look right at home in a container, or a modern or cottage garden.

OPPOSITE: *Lilium* 'American West' is one of the new "Orienpets," hybrids that combine the sweet, strong fragrance of Oriental lilies with the large blooms and sturdy stems of trumpet lilies.

"Simplify, simplify, simplify, with fewer but better choices. My plant addiction is still there, but now I need massive, pure doses that are unblended. Now it's tree peonies, bearded iris, and masses of white narcissus that deliver the kick I used to get from cannas, coleus, and colocasias. It seems everything old is new again. How modern is that?"

–Tom Hobbs, author, designer, proprietor of Southlands Nursery

understand rain and fog and snow and frost and sun in a visceral way we never did before we gardened. This interplay with nature is as consoling and comforting as plant lust is real.

But then, all too often, our relationship with our objects of adoration becomes a love-hate one. Just as with our human connections, what we first loved becomes what we most resent. Plants spread about; they need dividing and cutting back and staking. They grow far larger than we ever expected, casting dank shade over our gardens. The seasons follow each other so quickly, each with their myriad tasks, and we can never quite keep up. Our gardens become a burden, a drain, a series of chores, rather than the joy they once were—and can be again.

So the essential conundrum for gardeners is how to recapture the bliss of gardening while cutting down on all the work. Or, better yet, how to do it right the first time and make a garden that doesn't exhaust our energies and resources.

Short of running a cost-benefit equation (fragrance versus pruning, flavor versus fertilizer), the question comes down to how we can grow only the plants that give us the most satisfaction and gratification for money spent, ground given, and, most of all, time needed to care for them.

And yes, there are plenty of beautiful, gratifying plants that don't eat your garden or your life. Many bulbs are ideal for the simplified garden, as are small shrubs, dwarf conifers, petite trees, and less aggressive ground covers, and even some few roses and perennials.

The lists and descriptions in this chapter give you a framework for editing your plants so that each and every one gives you maximum pleasure for time and work invested. The goal is to not succumb to the "so many plants, so little time" mentality but instead to make sure that every plant you allow into your soil simplifies rather than complicates your gardening life.

All the plants listed in this chapter are considered to be hardy in USDA zones 6 through 9. If any plant is slightly more tender, it's noted in the description. But don't be daunted by the numbers, because even if you live in a colder climate than indicated, your garden may well offer microclimates hospitable enough to give these plants a try. None of these plants are temperamental, tender, tricky, or hard to care for. Be sure and vet every plant for your unique climate and growing conditions before you let it into your garden. And remember that any plant is only as good as the conditions in which you plant it. Even the most dependable, sturdy plant will flag or even die when planted in poor conditions.

To find photos of any of these plants, just google the plant name and then click "Images" at the top of the search results page to come up with a gallery of shots. Or invest in the most useful of books, *Right Plant, Right Place* by Nicola Ferguson (see "Resources"), which has more than a thousand color photos of plants, including all of the ones in these lists.

These plants aren't the newest, most exciting, most exotic, or coolest of the crop. However, using your own picks from these lists, you'll have all you need to plant a richly satisfying garden that pleases you without depleting you.

Pick of the Perennials

Perennials are change agents but require dividing, fertilizing, staking, deadheading, fussing around with. And what makes them exciting—their constant fluctuation through the seasons—means they need frequent tinkering, sequencing, staging, and just plain work. Many stop blooming and even collapse if not divided every year or so. You know those fabulous perennial borders you see in books? They only look that way because they've been plied with fertilizer and water, and cared for by a staff.

Yet most gardeners want a few perennials to fluff up the garden and herald seasonal change. There are literally thousands to choose from. Here's a sampling of the lowest-maintenance perennials around:

Aconitum napellus (monkshood) sports spikes of bright blue flowers in early summer so is a fine substitute for labor-intensive delphiniums. It takes some shade and needs dividing only once a decade.

Actea **(formerly** *Cimicifuga***)** *racemosa* **'Brunette'** (bugbane) has lacy dark leaves and sweetly fragrant flower spikes in autumn. You can leave it undisturbed for many years, just cutting back old foliage in winter.

Aquilegia (columbine) hybrids are old-fashioned charmers with intricate little flowers. They bloom year after year with little or no help from the gardener except clearing away the old foliage so fresh leaves can emerge.

Astrantia major **'Ruby Wedding'** or **'Hadspen Blood'** are tidy, clumping perennials smothered with curious little dark flowers that are surprisingly showy in the garden and last for weeks when cut for arrangements.

White flowers sweet smelling enough to scent the autumn garden are one reason to give bugbane garden room; the lacy, ebony foliage clinches the deal.

Hostas with fat, thickly ribbed foliage—like this mature clump of *Hosta sieboldiana* 'Elegans'—not only create a pleasing wavelike effect in the garden but also resist slugs and pests.

Bergenia **spp.** have big, paddle-shaped evergreen leaves that turn shades of purple and pink in winter. These are tough plants, ideal for rockeries, pots, or any place you want hardy, dependable foliage with a dramatic flair.

Helleborus orientalis hybrids have pretty winter blossoms in a range of colors, and leaves that persist all year. They bloom dependably at a time when not much else is happening out there, and their flowers are beguiling, in shades from white through yellow to darkest purple. They rarely need dividing, but in some gardens seed about too prolifically.

Heuchera **spp.** bred from the modest coral bells are foliage powerhouses that trim beds and fill pots. How did we garden before these new heucheras came on the scene? In some climates and conditions, their ruffled and variously colored foliages last through the winter. Some heucheras have proved more long lasting than others; auburn-toned 'Caramel' and 'Peach Flambe' and the dark 'Chocolate Ruffles' and 'Chocolate Veil', as well as the chartreuse 'Lime Rickey' and matte black 'Obsidian', are proving reliable.

Hosta **spp.** need slug and snail protection, as well as regular watering, but their great diversity of sizes and foliage colors is endlessly useful in the garden, and best of all they need dividing only once every ten years.

Miscanthus sinensis **'Gold Bar'** is an example of one of the many showy, easy-care ornamental grasses. It has a burst of gold-striped foliage topping out at only four feet, and hazy burgundy flowers in late autumn.

Paeonia **spp.** (peonies) offer not only lovely flowers but also handsome foliage. Leave them alone to grow and prosper, for they're deep-rooted, long-lived plants that greatly resent being moved or divided. They do require staking, but you might consider the twofer of foliage and flower worth the trouble.

The chartreuse foliage of *Hosta* 'Sum and Substance' is dramatically huge, and as a result of their heavy ribbing, the leaves are relatively slug and pest resistant.

For all its extravagant, showboating beauty, *Paeonia lactiflora* 'Bowl of Beauty' is extremely long lived and cold tolerant.

> "Whether plants are grown in great sophisticated sweeps or seductively jumbled jungles, we are now seeing gardens that truly reflect the vision of their creators. Contemporary gardens honor nature with the loving human hand as gentle shepherd rather than rigid dictator."
>
> —Steve Lorton, longtime Northwest bureau chief, Sunset magazine

Rodgersia **spp.** are shade and moisture lovers with handsome, pleated leaves that require little care besides irrigation and cutting back in late winter.

Sedum **'Autumn Joy'** and **'Summer Ice'** and the other tall sedums are hardy, drought tolerant, and beloved by butterflies, and need dividing only every five to ten years. Sedums are amazingly varied, they propagate and transplant easily, and you can't help but be drawn to their cunning shapes and stylish colors. In fact, if a visionary environmentalist-designer could have made up a whole category of plants to transform our gardening lives, it would be sedums.

Sedum 'Autumn Joy' spreads into a luxuriant stand of flat-topped pink-fading-to-buff flowers that'll carry on from July through frost, in the gallery garden of artists George Little and David Lewis.

Easy Ground Covers for Sun and Shade

Ground covers are by definition easy, for they spread to form a weed-suppressing, low-maintenance carpet. Some flower, others stand out for their scented, colorful, or textural foliage. All fill the bare-dirt void that weeds are all too happy to take advantage of.

Ground covers for a simplified garden must spread willingly but modestly, mingling with other ground covers to create a tapestry effect. You want to avoid ground covers that spread so aggressively they choke out other plants.

Always vet any recommended plant for your local conditions (Is it hardy? overly aggressive in my climate?) before planting. And for easy care, place ground covers a little more closely together than their spread at maturity so that they'll fill in quickly.

FOR SUN

Erigeron karvinskianus (Mexican fleabane) is both drought tolerant and delicate looking, with lacy, mounding foliage covered with daisylike little white flowers that keep on blooming for months.

Euphorbia myrsinites (donkey tail spurge) sprawls along the ground in ringlet-shaped stems of blue-green foliage that blooms chartreuse in springtime. It loves drought and sun, and needs only a snipping back in late autumn.

Festuca glauca (blue fescue) is one of the most carefree and striking of the ornamental grasses, for it takes to full sun and dry soil, and is hardy to zone 4. 'Elijah Blue' grows just eight inches high and has an especially rich silver-blue coloration.

A haze of blue fescue in full bloom thrives in the hot, dry conditions it loves best.

Fragaria spp., or strawberries—from the little sand strawberries (*F. chiloensis*) so tough they grow along the seacoast to the lusciously flowered *F.* 'Pink Panda' to edibles like musk strawberries (*F. moschata*)—are durable, handsome plants that deserve to be sprung from the vegetable patch and grown ornamentally.

Geranium **'Rozanne'** was chosen Perennial Plant of the Year for 2008 by the Perennial Plant Association for its long-blooming purple flowers and easy-care ways. Hardy geraniums have been called the "little black dress" of the garden, for they're dependable, easy, and work in nearly every situation and location.

Lavandula angustifolia (English lavender) evokes summer and the Mediterranean like nothing else, with its fragrant gray-green foliage and bee-and-butterfly-attracting purple flower wands. Hardy to zone 5, 'Hidcote' grows two feet tall; 'Munstead' is a bit shorter.

Pleioblastus viridistriatus (dwarf greenstripe bamboo) is a lawn alternative with chartreuse leaves striped in darker green ribbons. It can grow two to three feet high, but if you mow it down in winter it'll stay low growing and soft enough to be walked on. It's billed as hardy to 0 degrees F but lives through the winter, even in Minnesota. *P. viridistriatus* 'Chrysophyllus' is a stripeless solid chartreuse version. *Warning*: this is a running bamboo so is only low-maintenance when a twenty-four-inch-deep bamboo rhizome barrier is installed all around the perimeter of the bamboo planting to contain it.

Sedum '**Vera Jameson**' is one of many useful sedums ideal for sunny, droughty spots in the garden; this one is notable for its dark purple–bronze succulent foliage and creeping, low-growing habit. *S. spurium* 'Tricolor' is also a showy choice with pink, white, and green leaves.

Stachys byzantina '**Silver Carpet**' (lamb's ears) is a wooly silver-leafed plant that loves sun and arid conditions but grows happily just about anywhere. Children love its soft fuzziness; gardeners appreciate the contrast its silver sheen lends to any plant grouping. 'Silver Carpet' is lower maintenance than the species because it doesn't throw up tall purple blooming spikes that need to be cut off when they quickly look ratty; 'Primrose Heron' has a yellow cast to its gray leaves.

Stipa gigantea and *Stipa tenuissima* are two exceptionally lovely grasses, and for very different reasons. The former grows into a large mound that sends up tall wheat-colored blooms in June that last through summer. Mexican feather grass (*S. tenuissima*) is a bleached blonde little beauty with a tawny, filigreed appeal. Both hold up over a long season and require little care besides a yearly clipping. These two are somewhat tender (the former thrives in zones 8 through 10 and the latter in zones 7 through 10) but worth a try in well-drained soil even in zones that are slightly colder than recommended.

FOR SHADE

Ajuga reptans (bugleweed) is another familiar ground cover with exciting new cultivars, like 'Caitlin's Giant" with fat, dark purple leaves; tricolored 'Rainbow'; and dwarf, semi-sweet colored 'Chocolate Chip'.

The soft, feathery quality of
Stipa tenuissima is played up when
the plant is backlit by the
afternoon sun.

Carex **spp.** (sedges) are sturdy little evergreens that are easy-care gorgeous in the landscape and unsurpassed by any of the ornamental grasses for tidy form and year-round dependability. These textural bursts of color actually resent being cut back or watered too often, so leave them alone to grow to their foot-or-so-height, where they'll stay put and grace your garden for years, in pots or in the ground. Mix them together to cover the ground; there are many colors and textures to choose from. There's the bronze leatherleaf sedge *C. buchananii,* the shimmery silver *C. comans* 'Frosted Curls', the golden *C. alata* 'Aurea', and my all-time

The deceptively delicate looking tracery of an autumn fern's weatherproof bronzed foliage is shown off against a variegated hosta.

favorite, the orange New Zealand sedge *C. testacea* with foliage in glossy shades of copper and olive green. All take some sun but prefer at least partial shade.

Dryopteris erythrosora (autumn fern) is a dwarf evergreen fern with orange and coppery fronds that needs no more care than cutting back in spring so the new foliage can emerge.

Epimedium **spp.** are heart-shaped little ground covers that you can plant in your driest, most challenging shady areas, and they'll still thrive.

Hakonechloa macra '**Aureola**' (Japanese forest grass) is a deciduous grass but worth growing despite its absence in winter, for this is arguably the most beautiful of all the ornamental grasses. Its glowingly golden-striped foliage has a flowing liquid quality unlike any other plant. 'All Gold' is solid chartreuse; 'Albo Variegata' has white stripes.

Hostas are so useful and beautiful they're included here despite their need for water and their attractiveness to slugs that riddle their leaves with holes. Thicker-leafed types are more slug resistant, and if you have a naturally damp area in your garden no ground cover is more lovely. 'Sum and Substance' has giant chartreuse leaves; 'Ground Master', with green leaves trimmed in white, tops out under a foot tall.

Lamium maculatum (spotted dead nettle) is a well-behaved shade lover and an old-fashioned ground cover rejuvenated with fresh new cultivars. 'White Nancy' and 'Beacon Silver' have pale leaves rimmed in green, and 'Beedham's White' has chartreuse foliage. The little hooded flowers come in pink or white.

Liriope (lilyturf) is one of the most bulletproof of ground covers. It has the tufted look of ornamental grasses but with the added bonus of pretty flowers. It tolerates drought, heat, and humidity. *L. muscari* 'Big Blue' is evergreen, with lilac flowers in late summer; creeping lilyturf (*L. spicata*) grows only ten inches high, spreads quickly, and is hardy to zone 4 or 5.

Ophiopogon planiscapus '**Nigrescens**' (black mondo grass) is the coolest ground cover ever, with shiny, spidery black foliage. It's one of the truest black plants there is, and its ebony coloration shows off variegated foliage plants to perfection.

Sedum makinoi '**Ogon**' is the rare sedum that prefers partial shade; other than that it has all the virtues of its kind. This tiny chartreuse creeper is drought tolerant and grows willingly just about anywhere.

In a garden composition as effective and spare as a haiku, an autumnal katsura leaf rests in a spidery expanse of black mondo grass.

GROUND COVERS YOU CAN WALK ON

These ground covers are ideal lawn substitutes, for they take foot traffic, even if they're not quite uniform enough for a game of croquet. They are more textural and colorful than lawn grass, some are scented, and all are less thirsty and labor intensive than turf. Many are marketed under the trademarked name of "Stepables." Most are hardy to zones 5 or 6. Some, like blue star creeper and New Zealand brass buttons, are evergreen in warmer climates or warmer winters but in zones 6 and 7 may die back in winter and sprout again in springtime.

Achillea tomentosa (woolly yarrow) is a larger-textured choice, with fuzzy gray-green leaves and yellow flowers.

Chamaemelum nobile (chamomile) is a sweet-smelling ground cover with tiny leaves and yellow flowers.

Isotoma fluviatilis (blue star creeper) is a fine-textured but tough creeper with exceptionally pretty, long-lasting little pale blue flowers that give this beauty plenty of room to spread.

Leptinella squalida (New Zealand brass buttons) is one of the dwarfest ground covers, with feathery, fernlike foliage; 'Platt's Black' is most unusual with bronze-and-black foliage.

Mentha requienii (Corsican mint) prefers a little shade; it releases a strong minty scent when walked upon.

Japanese forest grass laps up against stone pavers outlined in blue star creeper for a summer-long contrast in color and texture.

'Platt's Black' New Zealand brass buttons hug the sides of this gravel path and provide a subtle texture in the garden, showing off paler or brighter plants like the yellow-striped phormiums.

Ophiopogon japonicus **'Nanus'** (mondo grass) is a tufty little dwarf grass that grows only a couple of inches high, creating a highly textured, modern look when massed to cover the ground. This one is on the tender side, for zones 7 through 10.

Sagina subulata (Irish moss) and **S. subulata 'Aurea'** (Scotch moss) are both lush looking and quick growing, perfect to plant around stepping-stones. Scotch moss is a bright chartreuse; Irish moss is emerald green.

Thymus praecox **'Pseudolanuginosus'** (woolly thyme) with its tiny, hairy gray-green leaves is one of the more drought-tolerant carpeters; it doesn't bloom much, which is good if you want to walk barefoot without stepping on bees, but if you want flowers, plant the cultivar 'Hall's Woolly', which blooms lavender-pink.

Easy Perennial Bulbs

Bulbs are the wizards of the garden, for all you do is stick a wrinkled brown lump in the ground in autumn, and up poke flowers the next spring. Seemingly invented for a simplified garden, bulbs that are wisely chosen and placed multiply and

spread to bring sheets of color to the spring garden, as with crocus and narcissus, or height and showy bloom to the summer garden, as with alliums and lilies.

Meet their exacting requirements, and bulbs perform generously. Choose types that are truly perennial and plant them in a sunny spot where the soil drains well, or in containers if your soil is waterlogged. Drainage is vital, for bulbs will rot in the ground if they get too wet over the winter. Give them what they need, and bulbs will reward you with year after year of glorious bloom.

Get this—bulbs are so "user friendly" that if you mistakenly plant them on their sides (they should be planted pointy end up), they right themselves underground into the proper growing position.

Bulbs look best planted in multiples, so buy as many as you can afford of a single kind and color and plant them closely together to get the best effect. You can plant in succession for waves of bloom, beginning with crocus in late winter, continuing through summer with statuesque, supremely fragrant Oriental lilies, and bookending in September with autumn crocus. Never plant in rows, plant in odd numbers, and plant plenty (but even a drift of five is lovely).

Alliums or ornamental onions throw leaves up first, followed by stems topped with balls of bloom in late May into June. These fat, round bursts of sophisticated flower grow up happily between shrubs. They'll be the most asked-about flower in your garden. *Allium* 'Globemaster' is one of the largest of its kind, with eight-to-ten-inch purple globes atop three-foot-tall stems. *A.* 'Purple Sensation' blooms first with more of a violet tinge, and Star of Persia (*A. christofii*) looks like a spaceship landed in the garden, with short stems and basketball-sized flower heads in shimmering lavender.

Colchicums bloom in autumn and look like crocuses on steroids. Oddly, their leaves appear in spring and die down, and then the flower pops up leaf-free, earning them the nickname of "naked ladies." Colchicums perform well in shade but do need perfect drainage like the rest of their relatives. *Colchicum cilicicum* is purplish-pink and honey scented, *C.* 'Waterlily' is the classic double lilac, and *C. speciosum* 'Album' is snow white and goblet shaped.

Crocuses are great naturalizers, blooming early and multiplying prolifically. Dig a shallow depression and throw in a handful for a casual, natural look, or layer them into your pots for early color. *Crocus tommasinianus* in shades of purple, lavender, and mauve are the first to bloom and are more squirrel resistant than most crocuses. *C. chrysanthus* 'Cream Beauty' is pale and plump with purple margins, and *C. vernus* 'Flower Record' is larger, with purple cups and orange stamens.

Daffodils (*Narcissus* spp.) have many virtues—they're the true harbingers of springtime with their early, sunny flowers, they return dependably year after year, many are scented, they make long-lasting cut flowers, and because they're poisonous, squirrels and other hungry varmints don't eat them. Their only drawback is the floppy foliage that needs to be left alone to die down and feed the bulb so it'll bloom next year. So pass up the largest trumpet daffodils and plant these smaller beauties with foliage that has less obvious death throes: Pheasant's eye or the poet's daffodil (*N.* 'Actea') has a pale cup with a yellow center outlined in orange, and a rich, spicy fragrance. Plant enough and it'll look like a flock of little white

Narcissus multiply and return every year to scent and brighten the early spring garden.

A single bulb of a lily as tall, fragrant, and luscious as these classic *Lilium* 'Anaconda' trumpets will turn any gardener into a lily worshiper.

doves has landed in your garden. *N.* 'Pink Charm' blooms a little earlier in shades of white, peach, and pink, *N.* 'Thalia' is pure white and strongly fragrant, and *N.* 'Tête-á-Tête' is tiny and bright gold.

Lilies are the fireworks of the summer garden, taking up little space in relation to the impact of their huge flowers. Tuck a fat lily bulb in the ground in autumn before the ground freezes, and in summer you'll have a stately miracle of a flower stalk sporting sublimely beautiful flowers with intoxicating scent. Lilies require only sun and good drainage; plant them in the right spot and they'll grow into an increasingly large and floriferous clump year after year. The new hybrid "Orienpets" are sturdy, fragrant, and disease resistant; among them, *Lilium* 'Golden Stargazer' is upward facing, golden, and lightly freckled, and *L.* 'Silk Road' is long blooming with nodding purple-and-white trumpet flowers. Oriental lilies are the Scarlett Johanssons of the plant world, almost too luscious to be believed with their huge, deliciously fragrant flowers, like the iconic white *L.* 'Casa Blanca' and the raspberry *L.* 'Star Gazer'.

Tulips are everyone's favorite, but most are not perennial, needing to be replanted every year for a good show. Some few tend to come back faithfully. Darwin hybrid tulips, when planted a foot deep, are the most long lasting and persistent of the tall tulips. *Tulipa* 'Okura' is vivid orange, 'Daydream' is apricot, and 'Jewel of Spring' is soft yellow edged in red. The little rock tulips, or Kaufmanniana hybrids, are the most dependable naturalizers in the tulip clan. They are low-growing with mottled foliage and look their best growing in rockeries, pots, or the front of the border. *T.* 'Heart's Delight' is rose and carmine-red; *T.* 'Early Harvest' is yellow and orange. Some of the little species tulips are also perennial, including the copper-colored *T. hageri* 'Splendens' and the yellow *T. kolpakowskiana*.

Small Shrubs Are Your Best Friends

Tidy little shrubs have eaten perennials' lunch, and for good reason—shrubs grow to their mature height and girth, and then they stay put. Shrubs contribute structure, color, bloom, scent, and berries to the garden, all with a minimum of care. Besides a bit of pruning and maybe a spring dose of compost and manure, they need no help from you to perform through the year.

Look for shrubs whose nature it is to stay a reasonable three-to-four-foot size, and others for which dwarf varieties have been developed. Each of the shrubs described here is petite enough to fit into borders or containers; if you have space, plant them in multiples. Most of these shrubs stay under five feet tall—none will surprise you years hence by growing into trees

EVERGREEN

Buxus microphylla **'Kingsville Dwarf'** (littleleaf boxwood) grows slowly to a three-foot-tall pincushion-shaped bump.

Chamaecyparis obtusa **'Gold Fern'**, a false cypress with fluffy, tawny-tipped branches, is only one of many dwarf conifers as rewarding as they are easy to care for. The blue Spanish fir *Abies pinsapo* 'Glauca' is a head turner, and the hemlock *Tsuga canadensis* 'Gentsch White' has branches that appear dipped in snow or powdered sugar.

Daphne **spp.**, with their rep for fickleness, may not seem to belong in this book, but if you can find a spot with perfect drainage, perhaps in a big pot, winter daphne (*Daphne odora* 'Marginata') is worth trying. If it's happy in its location, it's a carefree, sprawling shrub with cream-bordered leaves and achingly sweet-smelling early spring flowers. A little less persnickety is *Daphne ×transatlantica* 'Summer Ice', a four-foot mound of a shrub with white-trimmed leaves and tiny, fragrant flowers over a long season.

Mahonia aquifolium (Oregon grape) is larger than many of these shrubs, up to six feet tall, but well worth the garden room. It's sturdy and tough, with jagged toothed evergreen foliage and pale yellow wands of scented flowers in December. *Mahonia aquifolium* 'Compacta' grows to only two to three feet tall; all species have edible blue-black berries.

Nandina domestica (heavenly bamboo) is a lacy evergreen shrub not actually related to bamboo. It's a true four-season plant, with bronze-red spring foliage, trusses of creamy flowers in summer, and showy crimson berries in autumn to feed the birds. Nandinas aren't fussy about soil, don't require pruning to maintain their graceful shape, and can take shade, although their foliage colors up more brightly when they're grown in a sunny spot. The species grows eight feet tall, ideal as a specimen or for screening. Newer cultivars like 'Moon Bay' with lime

"In an age that is DIY, I hope that we will still have creative and original gardens and not paint-by-number ones."

– Maurice Horn,
co-proprietor,
Joy Creek Nursery

green foliage and 'Nana Purpurea' with purple winter foliage are more compact and sport vivid leaves that change colors through the seasons.

Osmanthus **spp.** are evergreen shrubs with fragrant flowers. *O. delavayi* has small, dark-green leaves and white, sweet-smelling flowers in March. The holly-leaf variety *Osmanthus heterophyllus* 'Goshiki' has toothed leaves bright with yellow variegation and is a fine holly substitute. These shrubs are a little more tender, hardy only to zone 7.

Rhododendron yakushimanum stays under four feet tall, with handsome leaves backed in fuzzy indementum and large flowers compared to the size of the plant.

Rosemary officinalis is a culinary rosemary with gray-green foliage and early spring flowers in varying shades of blue (the paler the blue, the hardier the rosemary). It comes in shapes from spikey upright to prostrate, and its foliage is deliciously scented and useful for cooking. 'Arp' and 'Hill Hardy' are the hardiest of the rosemaries; when given good drainage they survive in zone 6.

Sarcococca **spp.** (sweet box) have shiny evergreen leaves and supremely fragrant, tassel-like white flowers that bloom all winter, followed by a crop of black berries.

DECIDUOUS

Abelia xgrandiflora **'Rose Creek'** has foliage with a pink tint that turns golden in autumn, and light pink to white summer flowers.

Berberis thunbergii **'Crimson Pygmy'** is a purple-leafed barberry ideal for pots or trimming the edges of borders.

Callicarpa bodinieri **var.** *giraldii* **'Profusion'** (beautyberry) shines in winter, when its bare branches are coated in bright lavender berries that look as if spray painted with metallic gleam. Plant at least three in a tight cluster to get the full effect.

Caryopteris xclandonensis has arching branches coated in bright blue flowers from August to the first frost. 'Worcester Gold' has yellow foliage and lavender-blue flowers; 'Dark Knight' has silvery gray leaves and deep blue, long-lasting flowers.

Deutzia gracilis **'Nikko'** is a miniature version of the familiar shrub, with hundreds of tiny white flowers despite its diminutive size, growing only a foot high.

Fothergilla gardenii is a two-to-three-foot-high dwarf with white, fragrant bottlebrush flowers in spring and a blaze of brilliant yellow to scarlet fall color.

Spirea japonica '**Magic Carpet**' is an ideal small mound of a shrub with red-tipped yellow leaves that come on early to accent spring bulbs and that retain their bright color until late autumn. Other dwarf Japanese spirea include 'Alba', with white flowers and pale green leaves, and 'Limemound', with yellow-green leaves that turn intense orange in autumn.

Spirea japonica 'Magic Carpet' is a tidy little workhorse of a spirea with brilliant spring foliage that quiets to golden yellow in summer.

Weigela **spp.** fall into the "everything old is new again" category of familiar shrubs recently updated with flashier-foliaged varieties. *W.* 'Florida Variegata' has cream trim on the leaves, and the blatant *W.* 'Olympiade' has red flowers and golden leaves. All types have bell-shaped flowers beloved by hummingbirds.

Easy, Healthy Roses

The days of donning a moon suit to spray roses with poisons are so over. There's no good reason to grow demanding hybrid teas, but there's also no reason to do without the romance of roses in your garden. While you won't find the long-stemmed perfection of roses past on this list, you will find modern, fragrant shrub and ground cover roses that have attractive foliage, grow happily in pots and borders rather than rose ghettos, and can hold their own for durability and ease of care with any other plant on any of these lists.

"Easy Elegance" roses are a new, trademarked series marketed as "not your grandmother's roses." They're compact shrubs, great border minglers, hardy to zone 4, and are so disease resistant and easy to grow that they come with a two-year guarantee.

English roses, or David Austin roses, are bred to combine the virtues of old roses and modern roses. They have the fruity scents and overblown beauty of old-fashioned roses along with the nonstop bloom of hybrid teas. Many gardeners, however, haven't found them as disease resistant as hoped, but they're so beautiful and fragrant they're probably worth experimenting with.

"Knock Out" roses are a trademarked series of low-growing shrub roses. Hybridizer William Radler claims he's "breeding the maintenance out of roses" with this series. More than forty types offer a variety of sizes and flower colors and shapes, and need little watering and no spraying to stay healthy.

Rosa glauca is a species rose hardy to well below 0 degrees F, with a cascade of pewter-colored foliage. This is a rose grown for its uniquely colored leaves as much as for its pretty pink single blossoms and bright red hips, shown off so well by the blue-gray leaves.

Rosa **'Korwest'** (known more commonly by the trade name Westerland) is the only rose besides *Rosa glauca* that I've ever grown without a sign of blackspot. This ruffled apricot-orange floribunda is spicily fruit scented, holds up well in

Perhaps because of its simple, open flowers and unusual pewter-colored foliage, *Rosa glauca* looks as much at home in a spare, modern garden as in a more traditional one.

arrangements, and blooms profusely over many months, with healthy leaves and, unfortunately, wicked thorns.

Rosa mulliganii is a fragrant, vigorous climber, with single white blooms followed by orange hips. Its showers of flowers star at Sissinghurst's famous White Garden. This exceptionally healthy rose thrives on neglect and is hardy to zone 5.

Rugosa roses have handsome crinkled foliage and are the shrub to throw at your most difficult landscaping challenge. They're shade tolerant, disease resistant, extremely cold hardy, and can take wind and salt spray. Their old-fashioned flowers often repeat-bloom, followed by large and showy fruit. *Rosa* 'Hansa' has ruffled reddish-purple flowers that are deeply fragrant; *R.* 'Topaz Jewel' is the rare yellow rugosa that grows five feet high with fruit-scented semidouble blossoms. For smaller gardens, the "Pavement" series of rugosas are short and spreading, topping out under three feet high, and come in colors from snow white through candy pink to deep red.

Bamboos That Behave

Most gardeners are rightly scared of bamboos, for nature expresses her life force through them more strongly than through most plants. Yet no other plants offer

While *Himalayacalamus hookerianus* 'Teague's Blue' isn't the hardiest of clumping bamboos, it's a beauty well worth growing if you live in climates where winter temperatures stay above 15 degrees F.

such grace and delicacy but still grow in quickly to form a sturdy and dependable evergreen screen. Their profile is narrow, so they take up very little room in the garden while contributing practical height and screening as well as great rustling-in-the-wind atmospherics, edible canes, and bird habitat.

And now nurseries are carrying "bamboos that behave" (no, that's not an oxymoron). These clumping bamboos still spread but slowly into larger clumps, like iris, rather than sending out those treacherously aggressive rhizomes like the traveling bamboos. One woman's breeding program has made hardy, clumping bamboo available to gardeners. Jackie Heinricher, founder and CEO of Booshoot Gardens, is busy producing her well-behaved bamboos to ship around the world. Here are just a few of Heinricher's clumpers:

Borinda boliana is one of the first-ever-produced hardy timber bamboos. It's perfect for solving any privacy problems because it grows thirty to fifty feet tall, with powder-blue new canes that turn to burgundy and purple as they mature. The most cold-tolerant bamboo in this genus, it can survive temperatures down to 10 degrees F.

Chusquea culeou is a drought-tolerant, tight clumper that grows fifteen to eighteen feet tall and is hardy to between 0 and 15 degrees F.

Fargesia robusta has shiny olive-green leaves and geometric white patterning on the canes. Its narrow, clean habit makes it an ideal screening bamboo. While this most useful of bamboos is very hardy, down to −4 degrees F, it isn't recommended for sultry southeastern climate zones.

Fargesia rufa is dainty, topping out at eight feet, with orange-red cane sheaths. 'Sunset Glow' is an especially vivid and cold-hardy cultivar. Both make great screens or hedges. The species is hardy to −15 degrees F, and 'Sunset Glow' to −20 degrees F.

Himalayacalamus hookerianus **'Teague's Blue'** (blue bamboo) is a robust blue-toned clumper that grows fifteen to twenty feet tall. It isn't as hardy as some clumpers, surviving temperatures down to 15 degrees F. 'Baby Blue' is a more diminutive choice of equal hardiness.

Ten Top Trees

Choosing trees, and not too many of them, is quite literally the biggest plant decision you'll ever make. Nothing looks more innocent than a sweet little gallon-sized tree—but don't be taken in.

Visit local public gardens and arboreta to see the height and girth these trees reach in your climate. Consider their eventual shape, which is as important as flower, leaf, or needle. Does the tree spread to have a wide crown at maturity, have a tiered or narrow spear shape, or does it grow as fat as it does tall? The feel of your garden as well as what you can grow depends on the shade and shadow cast by the trees you plant today. The best thing you can do for yourself is to choose a tree that grows naturally into the size and shape that fits the spot and role you have in mind, so that all it'll ever need is a little pruning to open it up a bit. Trees that offer interest in at least three out of four seasons earn the considerable space they take up in the garden.

Some of the "trees" in my top-ten list are really large shrubs that over time grow treelike to form the canopy layer in urban and suburban-sized gardens.

EVERGREEN

Arbutus unedo (strawberry tree) has round red knobby fruits that appear at the same time as clusters of little white flowers in fall and winter. Cut a branch, stick it in a vase, and you have a holiday arrangement of leaf, fruit, and flower. A handsome broadleaf evergreen, strawberry tree has red-brown shredding bark reminiscent of a madrone's and is drought tolerant and slow growing. The species grows very slowly to eighteen feet high and wide; *A. unedo* 'Compacta' reaches only about six to ten feet. Hardy only to zone 7.

Chamaecyparis obtusa **'Nana Gracilis'** (dwarf hinoki cypress) is one of the finest small conifers with swirls and twirls of vivid deep green foliage. It grows very slowly to eight feet tall. *C. obtusa* 'Aurea' is taller, to fifteen feet, with golden foliage, while 'Split Rock' is more columnar with a blue tint to its handsome evergreen needles and grows slowly to thirty feet.

Cryptomeria japonica **'Elegans'** (Japanese cedar or plume cedar) is a fluffy, soft conifer that turns bronze in winter and greens back up in summer. It lends an airy effect to the garden for a conifer and grows slowly to fifteen or twenty feet, keeping its slim, columnar shape over the years.

Mahonia ×*media* '**Charity**' grows eight to ten feet high, with jagged evergreen foliage topped off with sprays of fragrant yellow flowers in winter. Hardy only to zone 7.

DECIDUOUS

Acer **spp.**, small maples like the vine maple (*Acer circinatum*) or the more delicate-looking *Acer palmatum* 'Moonfire', are as at home in a woodland setting as in smaller urban and suburban gardens. They offer a graceful tracery of handsome leaves and an elegant presence in the garden even when bare of foliage. Vine maples, often multitrunked, are tough little trees that thrive when grown in parking strips or beneath conifers. The diminutive, delicate-looking 'Moonfire' is exceptional for its dark red foliage that retains its deep color through the heat and sun of summer, turning crimson in autumn.

Cornus kousa (kousa dogwood) is a delicate, disease-free dogwood with white flowers that turn pink with age; a pleasing horizontal, layered growth habit; and vivid fruits in autumn.

Cotinus **spp.** (smoke bush) are rock-tough, drought-tolerant, gorgeous large shrubs or small trees. A variety of cultivars offer sweetly rounded leaves in shades of darkest purple, soft green, or gold as bright as Roman coins. In summer, smoke bushes earn their common name by blooming a haze of flowers. *Cotinus coggygria* 'Grace' is the largest-leafed purple type with blazing red fall color; *C. coggygria* 'Golden Spirit' glows chartreuse all summer long. Cut smoke bush down close to the ground in late winter every few years to keep the leaves larger and the shape bushier.

Malus **spp.** (crabapples), when selected for disease resistance, offer flowers, fruit, and fragrance without the problems that so often plague ornamental cherries. *Malus* 'Adirondack' is covered in coral fruit, its columnar shape works well in smaller gardens, and it tops out at eighteen feet high. *M.* 'Strawberry Parfait' has pale pink flowers and garnet-colored fruit; both are especially disease free.

Robinia pseudoacacia '**Frisia**' (golden locust) is beautiful only in summer, but its airy, filigreed leaves come on such a pure, vivid lemon yellow and hold their color so late into autumn that you won't mind. This is a tree you can let grow as big as it likes (to about twenty-five feet) and it'll only brighten rather than darken your garden.

A golden cotinus is vibrantly colored enough to enliven an entire corner of the garden over many months; cut it down to the ground every few years to keep the leaves large and lush.

Stewartia pseudocamellia (Japanese stewartia) has a pyramidal shape, tops out at twenty-five or thirty feet high, and sports large white flowers with fluffy yellow stamens in midsummer. It turns to a blaze of orange and scarlet in autumn, and in winter its bark has a rich, exfoliating red-and-brown patchwork effect.

Don't Plant This!

Some plants just don't suit a simplified garden. Many of these troublemakers are achingly desirable, with variegation, ruffled leaves, or pretty flowers to tempt you. But like that cute ruffian in high school you knew better than to date, these bad boys cause more trouble than they're worth.

These are plants that don't deserve the space they take up, let alone the time and effort to care for them. Some grow too big, too fast, for most city or suburban gardens. Others are genetically programmed to colonize or sucker, are messy, tend toward disease, have poisonous sap, or are slug, snail, or deer magnets. We all develop our own lists of plants to avoid, depending on where and in what conditions we garden, but there are some universal thugs that act up in gardens almost everywhere.

In some circumstances, like safely corralled in a pot, some of these plants may well be reasonably carefree additions to your garden. For instance, I love the fragrant (some might say stinky) tricolor leaves of the *Houttuynia cordata* 'Chameleon', but I've learned the hard way that it chokes out everything around it and is nearly impossible to eradicate if you plant it in the ground. So now I grow houttuynia only in a container where its green, cream, and watermelon–colored leaves are close to hand to clip for flower arrangements but can't spread about. I've even resorted to growing gooseneck loosestrife (*Lysimachia clethroides*) at the top of a slope in much drier soil than it would prefer so that I can enjoy the curious shape of its flowers without worrying about its invasive tendencies.

Unless you're prepared to spend time and effort to negotiate conditions with the following troublemakers, they deserve subtraction from, rather than addition to, your garden.

Aegopodium podagraria '**Variegatum**' (variegated bishop's weed or goutweed) has attractive green-and-cream leaves and can grow anywhere, but this doesn't mean you should ever plant this ground cover, for it spreads like crazy and is nearly impossible to eradicate once it gets a toehold in your garden.

Ampelopsis brevipedunculata (porcelain berry) is listed as an invasive in some areas of the country and spreads far too rapidly almost everywhere, making you wonder why this vigorous woody vine is still sold.

Buddleia davidii (butterfly bush) not only grows big and gangly and seeds itself about the garden but also escapes cultivation to invade wild areas. Cultivars of butterfly bush don't appear to cause such problems, nor do some of the other species such as *Buddleia globosa*, with round, orange clusters of fragrant flowers.

Daphne laureola (spurge laurel) is let into gardens by people expecting it to be a lovely fragrant shrub like its relatives. But in truth this is a noxious weed, spread about widely by rodents and birds, difficult to eradicate, with leaves, berries, and bark that are poisonous to cats, dogs, and humans. Even touching it can cause a rash.

Hedera helix (English ivy) is beloved by rats who live in its tangle, and even worse, it escapes gardens to colonize parks and woodlands. The variegated, smaller-leafed types of ivy haven't proven to be problematic.

Heracleum mantegazzianum (giant hogweed) is in the cow parsley family, and is a big, bold plant once considered ornamental. However, pretty looks belie its danger, for its clear-watery sap is a toxin that causes photodermatitis. If you get even a drop on your skin that's exposed to sunlight, burning blisters develop followed by purplish scars.

Phalaris arundinacea **var.** *picta* (variegated ribbon grass) is a devil of a spreader even in shade, so beware of this oh-so-pretty grass, or keep it confined to a pot.

Prunus laurocerasus (English laurel) is so dark and bulky it feels like a storm cloud descending on the garden, plus it grows so quickly and thickly it's a continual pruning problem. There's a good reason planting English laurel has been called an act of aggression.

Rhus typhina (staghorn sumac), **Himalayan honeysuckle** (*Leycesteria formosa*), and other such beauties sucker or seed about so aggressively that you're fighting them more than enjoying them.

Vinca major or *Vinca minor* (myrtle or periwinkle), whether large- or small-leafed, is the most common of ground covers, as boring as it is too aggressive.

Keep It Simple

I've drawn from the lists in this chapter to compile what I call the Simplified Seven: wonder plants that give you all that's needed to create a nearly indestructible landscape wherever you live. From ground cover to canopy, these few plants will clothe your garden in colorful leaves, lend flower and fragrance in several seasons, and take care of themselves as much as any living thing is able to. All of these easy-care, high-performance plants are hardy survivors, each so beautiful you'd never guess how tough it is.

THE SIMPLIFIED SEVEN

1. heavenly bamboo
2. sedges
3. sedums
4. lilies
5. smoke bush
6. autumn fern
7. fragrant sweet box

Add to this basic list a few pots of vegetables or herbs for cooking, fill a window box with summer flowers, and mix in a few native plants to attract and nourish birds and butterflies, and you'll have a fully fleshed-out garden. Or repeat the Simplifed Seven as needed for a garden that's as rewarding as it is easy to care for.

Resources

BOOKS

Covering Ground: Unexpected Ideas for Landscaping with Colorful, Low-Maintenance Ground Covers by Barbara W. Ellis (Storey, 2007). The glorious photos in this book will convince readers that ground covers, through careful choice and good design, can transcend their usual utilitarian role to be a rich, textural feature in any garden, whether formal or naturalistic.

Flora: A Gardener's Encyclopedia by Sean Hogan (Timber Press, 2003). More than twenty thousand plants fill the pages of this two-volume omnibus of gardening, making it the go-to encyclopedia for descriptions and photos of more

Agave parryi in pipelike cylindrical pots looks clean and modern. Despite its tropical looks, this hardy succulent can take winter temperatures that dip all the way down to 0 degrees F. Give it a sunny spot and it needs no care besides a rare watering.

plants than you ever imagined existed in this world. If you have these volumes, a local gardening book, and an Internet connection, you're all set.

Gardening with Conifers by Adrian Bloom (Firefly Books, 2002). This book is a testament to the fact that conifers can consort harmoniously with perennials, ornamental grasses, shrubs, and bulbs as part of the larger garden.

Hardy Succulents for Every Climate by Gwen Kelaidis (Storey, 2008). An encouraging look, with inspiringly beautiful photos, at the many diverse succulents that are dependably hardy.

Right Plant, Right Place: Over 1,400 Plants for Every Situation in the Garden, revised and updated, by Nicola Ferguson (Simon and Schuster, 2005). If you're only going to buy one gardening book, this is it, for this photo-filled tome is about as close as you'll ever get to a one-stop reference on plants. A thousand photos matched with even more descriptions of plants, all arranged by where a plant should be placed, and its attributes.

ONLINE RESOURCES

B&D Lilies, www.lilybulb.com. Check out this site for a complete lesson in all things lily and order a catalog for even more information.

Booshoot Gardens, www.booshootgardens.com, gives a wealth of information about bamboo and how to care for it.

Brent and Becky's Bulbs, www.brentandbeckysbulbs.com. If you have questions about the best kind of bulbs for your garden situation, check out the handy search tool on this Web site. You can search by color, bloom time, sun versus shade, height, flowering time, and deer and rodent resistance, as well as buy a great assortment of healthy bulbs.

David Austin Roses, www.davidaustinroses.com. David Austin is a busy man—I had no idea he had bred so many gorgeous roses. You'll find luscious photos and lists of which English roses are the most fragrant, toughest, most suitable for organic growing, and so forth, at this well-designed site.

Easy Elegance Rose Collection, www.easyeleganceroses.com. While this Web site is mostly a sales tool, it'll help you sort through the many different kinds of easy new roses, and includes a retailer list to help you locate them.

Great Plant Picks, www.greatplantpicks.org, is produced by Seattle's Miller

Botanical Garden, yet its photos and plant descriptions are handy for gardeners in any climate.

High Country Gardens, www.highcountrygardens.com, produces a monthly e-zine newsletter, which they'll be happy to deliver to your e-mail inbox. It's filled not only with color photos and plant possibilities, but also with reliable information on water-wise gardening with tough, drought-tolerant plants.

Knock Out Roses, www.knockoutroses.com. More utilitarian than beautiful, this site helps sort out the many new colors and kinds of ground-cover roses.

Monrovia's Web site, www.monrovia.com, is about as stylish a site as you'll find, rich with growing information, photos, and design help. Even if you live in a cold climate, there's so much current information on the site it'll make up for any frustration that you can't grow the more tender plants sold by California-based Monrovia.

Stepables, www.stepables.com. This site is all about clever marketing, but there are plenty of photos plus sound information on ground covers to be found in the sales pitch.

www.bulb.com and **www.bulbvideo.com** are sites with lots of quick, current information on choosing and growing bulbs.

Allium christofii is a shorter, stockier allium, with a starry lavender sphere-shaped flower the size of a small basketball. These wonderous-looking bulbs bloom dependably year after year in sun and well-drained soil.

Mossy urns and water pots holding

horsetails and papyrus anchor

one corner of the courtyard, lending

an aged air to the garden's simple,

modern lines.

INDEX

OPPOSITE: The appropriately named blue finger (*Senecio mandraliscae*) edges the driveway, with the large soft-looking leaves of *Agave attenuata* behind.

GARDEN CREDITS

Grateful thanks to all of the garden owners and designers represented by the photographs in this book and listed here.

Pages 1, 42 (bottom), 176, 194–199: Pfeiffer-Klein garden, David Pfeiffer design, Vashon Island, WA

Pages 2–3, 217 (top), 220, 227 (left): Sekhri garden, Jeong Hyeon Lee design, San Francisco, CA

Pages 5, 41, 151, 153–156: Smith garden, Shirley Alexandra Watts design, Berkeley, CA

Pages 6, 234–235: Durocher-Nelson garden, Withey Price design, Seattle, WA

Pages 7 (left), 87, 93, 245: Hoppin garden, Ted Hoppin design, Bainbridge Island, WA

Pages 7 (right), 92, 105 (top), 106: Flotree garden, Cameron Scott/Exteriorscapes design, Seattle, WA

Pages 10–33, 113, 162, 224 (top right), 229–230, 236, 250, 252: Easton garden, Richard Hartlage of AHBL and Katie Easton of Abrahams Architects design, Whidbey Island, WA

Pages 34–35, 58 (right), 59–60: Holden-Moll garden, Cevan Forristt design, San Jose, CA

Pages 36, 61–62, 268–269: Kaplan garden, Allworth Design and Nussbaum Group design and installation, Seattle, WA

Pages 37, 63–67, 249: Hall-Behrens garden, Lauren Hall-Behrens design, Portland, OR

Pages 39, 152, 258: Pleasure garden, Shirley Alexandra Watts design, San Francisco, CA

Pages 40, 94, 146–147: David Pfeiffer design, Kenmore, WA

Pages 42 (top), 57, 58 (left): O'Neill-Soper garden, Cevan Forristt design, Palo Alto, CA

Pages 43–47: Farrell-Easton garden, Katie Easton design, Seattle, WA

Page 45 (top): Davis garden, Zen Japanese Landscape design, Seattle, WA

Pages 48–53: Shimizu garden, Osamu Shimizu design, Glen Echo, MD

Pages 54–56, 126: Bennett garden, Vanessa Kuemmerle design, San Francisco, CA

Pages 68–70, 81, 95: Smith garden, Allworth Design and Nussbaum Group design and installation, Seattle, WA

Pages 72–74: Gee-Smith garden, Mitchell Smith Design Build, Seattle, WA

Pages 75, 229 (top right): Lee-Ballinger garden, Jeong Hyeon Lee design, San Francisco, CA

Pages 76–77, 84–85, 165, 270: Lloyd-Butler garden, Jeong Hyeon Lee design, San Francisco, CA

Page 79: Matthews garden, Gillian Matthews design, Seattle, WA

Pages 80, 159: Wittenstein garden, Melissa Clark design, Bethesda, MD

Pages 91, 96, 188–189, 243, 248: Cathy Sarkowsky garden, Scott Mantz design, Vashon Island, WA

Pages 97, 246: Holmes-Bonder garden, Melissa Clark design, Washington, DC

Pages 98, 215, 217 (bottom), 224 (top left), 225 (left), 229 (top left), 231 (bottom), 247: Elisabeth C. Miller Botanical Garden, Seattle, WA

Pages 99–101: Salon garden, Marlene Salon design, Portland, OR

Pages 106 (bottom), 107–108: Cameron Scott design, Seattle, WA

Pages 109, 111, 144 (top): Marquis garden, Whidbey Island, WA

Pages 110, 112, 172, 186 (bottom), 190–192: Caine garden, Cameron Scott/Exteriorscapes design, Seattle, WA

Pages 116–120, 130–131: Bedner-Ostrowski garden, Tom Mannion design, Arlington, VA

Pages 125: Kamera garden, Cheryl and Dennis Kamera design, Whidbey Island, WA

Pages 132, 137–141: Carlson garden, Jennifer Carlson design, Seattle, WA

Pages 133, 166, 187, 200–203, 227 (right): Useless Bay Coffee Company garden,

Elaine Michaelides design, Whidbey Island, WA

Pages 148, 173, 177, 183: Matlock-Johnson garden, Sylvia Matlock/DIG Nursery design, Vashon Island, WA

Pages 149, 158, 266: Bruns-Middaugh garden, Withey Price design, Bainbridge Island, WA

Pages 150, 240: Balkind-Le Gall garden, Melissa Clark design, Chevy Chase, MD

Pages 170–171, 174, 178, 181–182: Creasy garden, Rosalind Creasy design, Los Altos, CA

Page 184: Nichols Garden Nursery, Rose Marie Nichols McGee design, Albany, OR

Pages 186 (top), 207, 214, 222–223, 225 (right), 226 (left), 232: Pots for Ravenna Gardens, Barbara Libner design, Seattle, WA

Pages 212–213, 218: Margard garden, Withey Price design, Seattle, WA

Pages 216, 226 (right), 228, 241 (bottom): Prindle garden, Judith Prindle design, Whidbey Island, WA

Pages 219, 221: Davis garden, Julie Davis design, Seattle, WA

Pages 224 (bottom), 231 (top): Crooks garden, Stacie Crooks design, Shoreline, WA

Page 242: The Garden of Little and Lewis, Bainbridge Island, WA